# Uncovering Student Thinking
## About **Mathematics**
### in the **Common Core**

High School

*To my husband, Corey. Words can't describe my gratitude for your endless love, patience, and support.*

—Cheryl

*To all my students, you have taught me much more than I have taught you, and especially to my daughters Liz and Kate, I love you both bushels and pecks and hugs around the neck.*

—Carolyn

# Uncovering Student Thinking
## About Mathematics
## in the Common Core

**High School**

25 Formative Assessment Probes

## Cheryl Rose Tobey
## Carolyn B. Arline

CORWIN

A SAGE Company

CORWIN
A SAGE Company

FOR INFORMATION:

Corwin

A SAGE Company

2455 Teller Road

Thousand Oaks, California 91320

(800) 233-9936

www.corwin.com

SAGE Publications Ltd.

1 Oliver's Yard

55 City Road

London EC1Y 1SP

United Kingdom

SAGE Publications India Pvt. Ltd.

B 1/I 1 Mohan Cooperative Industrial Area

Mathura Road, New Delhi 110 044

India

SAGE Publications Asia-Pacific Pte. Ltd.

3 Church Street

#10-04 Samsung Hub

Singapore 049483

Acquisitions Editor:   Jessica Allan

Associate Editor:   Kimberly Greenberg

Editorial Assistant:   Cesar Reyes

Production Editor:   Melanie Birdsall

Copy Editor:   Gillian Dickens

Typesetter:   C&M Digitals (P) Ltd.

Proofreader:   Wendy Jo Dymond

Indexer:   Molly Hall

Cover Designer:   Anupama Krishnan

Printed in the United States of America

*Library of Congress Cataloging-in-Publication Data*

Tobey, Cheryl Rose, author.

Uncovering student thinking about mathematics in the common core, high school : 25 formative assessment probes / Cheryl Rose Tobey, Carolyn B. Arline.

pages cm

Includes bibliographical references and index.
ISBN 978-1-4522-7657-1 (pbk.)

1. Mathematics—Study and teaching (Secondary) 2. Mathematical ability—Evaluation. 3. Individualized instruction. 4. Effective teaching. I. Arline, Carolyn B., author. II. Title.

QA11.2.T63 2014
510.71'273—dc23          2013040942

This book is printed on acid-free paper.

FSC
www.fsc.org

MIX
Paper from responsible sources
FSC® C014174

14 15 16 17 18 10 9 8 7 6 5 4 3 2 1

# Contents

# Preface

# Mathematics Assessment Probes

## OVERVIEW

Formative assessment informs instruction and supports learning through varying methods and strategies aimed at determining students' prior knowledge of a learning target and using that information to drive instruction that supports each student in moving toward understanding of the learning target. Questioning, observation, and student self-assessment are examples of instructional strategies educators can incorporate to gain insight into student understanding. These instructional strategies become *formative assessments* if the results are used to plan and implement learning activities designed specifically to address the specific needs of the students.

This book focuses on using short sets of diagnostic questions, called Mathematics Assessment Probes. The Probes are designed to elicit prior understandings and commonly held misunderstandings and misconceptions. This elicitation allows the educator to make sound instructional choices, targeted at a specific mathematics concept and responsive to the specific needs of a particular group of students.

> Diagnostic assessment is as important to teaching as a physical exam is to prescribing an appropriate medical regimen. At the outset of any unit of study, certain students are likely to have already mastered some of the skills that the teacher is about to introduce, and others may already understand key concepts. Some students are likely to be deficient in prerequisite skills or harbor misconceptions. Armed with this diagnostic information, a teacher gains greater insight into what to teach. (McTighe & O'Connor, 2005)

The Mathematics Assessment Probes provided here are tools that enable high school teachers to gather important insights in a practical way and that provide immediate information for planning purposes.

## AUDIENCE

The first collection of Mathematics Assessment Probes and the accompanying Teacher Notes were written for the busy classroom teacher eager for thoughtful, research-based diagnostic assessments focused on learning difficulties and aimed at enhancing the effectiveness of mathematics instruction. Since the publication of the first three *Uncovering Student Thinking in Mathematics* resources (Rose & Arline, 2009; Rose, Minton, & Arline, 2007; Rose Tobey & Minton, 2011), we have continually received requests for additional probes. Both teachers and education leaders have communicated the need for a collection of research-based probes that focus on a narrower grade span. In addition to additional probes for each grade span, educators were eager for an alignment of the probes to the Common Core Mathematics Standards (Council of Chief State School Officers, 2010). In response to these requests, we set to work writing, piloting, and field testing a more extensive set of probes for high school teachers with a focus on targeting mathematics concepts within the new standards. This book is one in a series of *Uncovering* resources for the K–2, 3–5, 6–8, and 9–12 grade spans.

## ORGANIZATION

This book is organized to provide readers with the purpose, structure, and development of the Mathematics Assessment Probes as well as to support the use of applicable research and instructional strategies in mathematics classrooms.

Chapter 1 provides in-depth information about the process and design of the Mathematics Assessment Probes along with the development of an action-research structure we refer to as a QUEST Cycle. Chapters 2 through 6 contain the collection of probes categorized by concept strands with accompanying Teacher Notes to provide the specific research and instructional strategies for addressing students' challenges with mathematics. Chapter 7 highlights instructional considerations and images from practice to illuminate how easily and in how many varied ways the probes can be used in mathematics classrooms. This chapter also highlights how use of the probes can support students' proficiency with the Common Core's Mathematical Practices.

# Acknowledgments

We would like to thank the many mathematics educators who, during attendance at various professional development sessions, gave valuable feedback about features of the Probes, including structures, concepts to target, and purposes of use. Your excitement during these sessions is what continues to motivate us to develop and pilot additional probes and teacher notes.

We especially would like to acknowledge the contributions of the following educators who provided ideas and field-tested Probes, gave feedback on Teacher Notes, scheduled classroom administrations, and/or opened their classrooms to us to try Probes or interview students: Erica Cooper, Dwayne Elm, Robyn Graziano, Kendra Guiou, Julie Hernandez, Lori Libby, Melanie Maroy, Michelle Parks, Debbie Sheridan, Frank Smith, Kimarie Soule, Beverly Wentworth, and the middle and high school teachers of Maine's Regional School Unit 2 (RSU 2).

We would like to thank our Corwin editor, Jessica Allan, for her continued support and Senior Project Editor, Melanie Birdsall, for her dedication in helping us to bring our vision of the contents of these resources through to production. As before, we acknowledge Page Keeley, our science colleague, who designed the process for developing diagnostic assessment Probes and who tirelessly promotes the use of these assessments for formative assessment purposes, helping to disseminate our work in her travels.

Mostly, we are grateful for the continued support, sacrifice, and patience shown by our families—Corey, Grandad, Carly, Jimmy, Bobby, Samantha, and Jack; and Liz, Kate, Adam, Sophie, and Gram—throughout the writing of this final book in the series.

## PUBLISHER'S ACKNOWLEDGMENTS

Corwin gratefully acknowledges the contributions of the following reviewers:

Lyneille Meza
Coordinator of Data
   and Assessment
Denton ISD
Denton, TX

Randy Wormald
Math Teacher
Kearsarge Regional
   High School
Sutton, NH

# About the Authors

**Cheryl Rose Tobey** is a senior mathematics associate at Education Development Center (EDC) in Massachusetts. She is the project director for Formative Assessment in the Mathematics Classroom: Engaging Teachers and Students (FACETS) and a mathematics specialist for Differentiated Professional Development: Building Mathematics Knowledge for Teaching Struggling Students (DPD); both projects are funded by the National Science Foundation (NSF). She also serves as a director of development for an Institute for Educational Science (IES) project, Eliciting Mathematics Misconceptions (EM2). Her work is primarily in the areas of formative assessment and professional development.

Prior to joining EDC, Tobey was the senior program director for mathematics at the Maine Mathematics and Science Alliance (MMSA), where she served as the co–principal investigator of the mathematics section of the NSF-funded Curriculum Topic Study, and principal investigator and project director of two Title IIa state Mathematics and Science Partnership projects. Prior to working on these projects, Tobey was the co–principal investigator and project director for MMSA's NSF-funded Local Systemic Change Initiative, Broadening Educational Access to Mathematics in Maine (BEAMM), and she was a fellow in Cohort 4 of the National Academy for Science and Mathematics Education Leadership. She is the coauthor of six published Corwin books, including three prior books in the *Uncovering Student Thinking* series (2007, 2009, 2011), two *Mathematics Curriculum Topic Study* resources (2006, 2012), and *Mathematics Formative Assessment: 75 Practical Strategies for Linking Assessment, Instruction and Learning* (2011). Before joining MMSA in 2001 to begin working with teachers, Tobey was a high school and middle school mathematics educator for 10 years. She received her BS in secondary mathematics education from the University of Maine at Farmington and her MEd from City University in Seattle. She currently lives in Maine with her husband and blended family of five children.

**Carolyn B. Arline** is a secondary mathematics educator, currently teaching high school students in Maine. She also works as a teacher leader in the areas of mathematics professional development, learning communities, assessment, systematic school reform, standards-based teaching, learning and grading, student-centered classrooms, and technology. She has previously worked as a mathematics specialist at the Maine Mathematics and Science Alliance (MMSA) and continues her work with them as a consultant. Carolyn is a fellow of the second cohort group of the Governor's Academy for Science and Mathematics Educators and serves as a mentor teacher with the current cohort. She participated as a mathematics mentor in the National Science Foundation–funded Northern New England Co-Mentoring Network (NNECN) and continues her role as a mentor teacher. She serves as a board member of the Association of Teachers of Mathematics in Maine (ATOMIM) and on local curriculum committees. Carolyn received her BS in secondary mathematics education from the University of Maine.

# 1

# Mathematics Assessment Probes

To differentiate instruction effectively, teachers need diagnostic assessment strategies to gauge their students' prior knowledge and uncover their misunderstandings. By accurately identifying and addressing areas of difficulties, teachers can help their students avoid becoming frustrated and disenchanted with mathematics and can prevent the perception that "some people just aren't good at math." Diagnostic strategies also support instruction that builds on individual students' existing understandings while addressing their identified difficulties. Targeting specific areas of difficulty—for example, the transition from reasoning about whole numbers to understanding numbers that are expressed in relationship to other numbers (decimals and fractions)—enables teachers to perform focused and effective diagnostic assessment (National Research Council, 2005, p. 310). The Mathematics Assessment Probes in this book allow teachers to target specific areas of difficulty as identified in research on student learning.

The Probes typically include a prompt or question and a series of responses designed specifically to elicit prior understandings and commonly held misunderstandings that may or may not be uncovered during an instructional unit. In the example in Figure 1.1, students are asked to choose yes or no as well as to write about how they determined their answer choice.

**Figure 1.1**   Example of a Probe: Is It a Parallelogram? (Items A–D)

## Is It a Parallelogram?

| Circle Yes or No. | Explain your choice. |
|---|---|
| A. 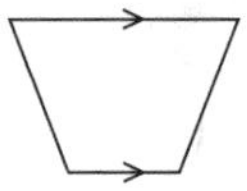 <br><br> Yes        No | |
| B. 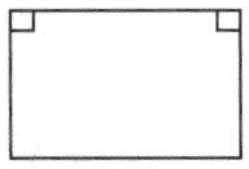 <br><br> Yes        No | |
| C. 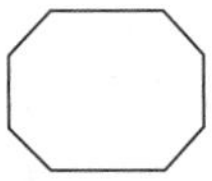 <br><br> Yes        No | |
| D. 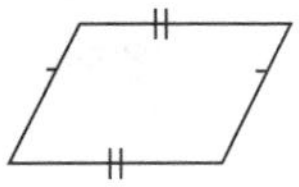 <br><br> Yes        No | |

Are you wondering about the Probes? If you are, we suggest reviewing the following Probes as initial examples:

- Simplifying Rational Expressions, p. 61
- Logarithms, p. 126
- Trigonometric Ratios, p. 159

This combination of selected response and further explanation helps to guide teachers in making instructional choices based on the specific needs of students. Since not all Probes follow the same format, we will discuss the varying formats later in this chapter. If you are wondering what other kinds of Probes are included in this book, take a few moments to review two or three additional Probes from Chapters 2 to 6 before continuing reading, but we strongly suggest that you return to read the rest of this chapter before beginning to use the Probes with your students.

At this point, you may be asking, "What is the difference between Mathematics Assessment Probes and other assessments?" Comprehensive diagnostic assessments for mathematics such as Northwest Education Association (NWEA) and Galileo Online (Assessment Technologies, Inc.), as well as the many state- and district-developed assessments, can provide information important for finding entry points and current levels of understanding within a defined progression of learning for a particular mathematics subdomain such as expressions and equations. Such assessments will continue to play an important role in schools because they allow teachers to get a snapshot of student understanding across multiple subdomains, often at intervals throughout the year depending on the structure of the assessment.

How are Probes different from these other assessments? Consider the following vignette:

> In a high school geometry class, students first complete the Is It a Parallelogram? Probe individually. Next, small groups of students discuss and reconcile their different ideas about whether the information provided about a figure is sufficient to determine whether that figure is a parallelogram. With the goal of consensus, students within each group justify their choice, trying to persuade others who disagree. As each group works to produce justifications that will be shared with the whole class, the teacher circulates among the group, probing further and encouraging argumentation. At the end of class, students are asked to revisit their initial responses and are provided time to revise their choices and explanations. The teacher uses this information to prepare for the next day's lesson. (Excerpt adapted from Keeley & Rose Tobey, 2011)

The Is It a Parallelogram? Probe in this vignette serves as a diagnostic assessment at several points during the lesson. The individual elicitation allows the teacher to diagnose students' current understanding; the conversations about sufficient evidence both build the teacher's understanding of what students are thinking and create a learning experience for students to further develop their understanding of the properties of parallelograms. The individual time allotted for revising responses allows the teacher to assess whether students are able to integrate this new knowledge with former conceptions or whether additional instruction or intervention is necessary.

Rather than addressing a variety of math concepts, Probes focus on a particular subconcept within a larger mathematical idea. By pinpointing one subconcept, the assessment can be embedded at the lesson level to address conceptions and misconceptions while learning is under way, helping to bridge from diagnostic to formative assessment.

Helping all students build understanding in mathematics is an important and challenging goal. Being aware of student difficulties and the sources of those difficulties, as well as designing instruction to diminish them, are important steps in achieving this goal (Yetkin, 2003). The process of using a Probe to diagnose student understandings and misunderstandings and then responding with instructional decisions based on the new information is the key to helping students build their mathematical knowledge. Let's take a look at the complete Probe implementation process we call the *QUEST Cycle* (also see Figure 1.2):

- **Q**uestioning Student Understanding: Determine the key mathematical understandings you want students to learn.
- **U**ncovering Student Understanding: Use a Probe to uncover understandings and areas of difficulties.
- **E**xamining Connections to Research and Educational Literature: Prepare to answer the question, "In what ways do your students' understandings relate to those described in the research base?"
- **S**urveying the Student Responses: Analyze student responses to better understand the various levels of understanding demonstrated in their work.
- **T**eaching Implications: Consider and follow through with next steps to move student learning forward.

**Figure 1.2** QUEST Cycle

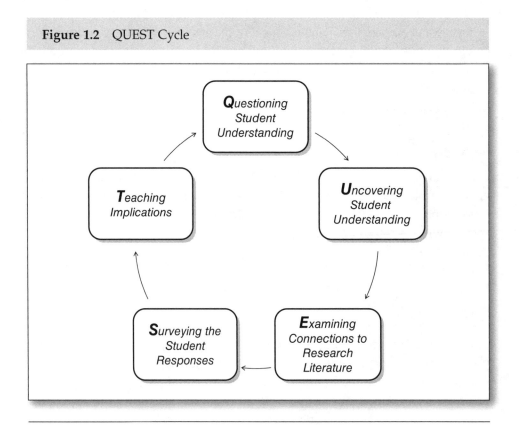

*Source:* Adapted from Rose, Minton, and Arline (2007).

Notice that in the Is It a Parallelogram? vignette, this cycle is repeated several times within the described instructional period.

The remaining parts of this chapter describe important components of the QUEST Cycle for implementing Probes, including background information on the key mathematics, the structure of the Probes, and connections to the research base. In addition, you will learn about how to get started with administering the Probes.

## QUESTIONING STUDENT UNDERSTANDING: DETERMINE THE KEY MATHEMATICAL CONCEPTS YOU WANT STUDENTS TO LEARN

The Common Core Standards for Mathematics (referred to as the Common Core or CCSM) define what students should understand and are the basis of the targeted mathematics concepts addressed by the Probes in this book. These understandings include both conceptual knowledge and procedural knowledge, both of which are important for students' mathematical development.

> Research has strongly established that proficiency in subjects such as mathematics requires conceptual understanding. When students understand mathematics, they are able to use their knowledge flexibly. They combine factual knowledge, procedural facility, and conceptual understanding in powerful ways. (National Council of Teachers of Mathematics [NCTM], 2000, p. 20)

Think about the experience of following step-by-step driving directions to an unfamiliar destination using the commands of a GPS but never having viewed a road map of the area. Although it may be easy to follow the directions one step at a time, if you lose your satellite reception, you will likely not know where to turn next or even which direction to head. Using a GPS without a road map is like learning procedures in math without understanding the concepts behind those procedures. Learners who follow the steps of a mathematical procedure without any conceptual understanding connected to that procedure may get lost when they make a mistake. Understanding the bigger picture enables learners to reason about a solution and/or reconstruct a procedure.

This relationship between understanding concepts and being proficient with procedures is complex. Table 1.1 provides some examples of each type of understanding for a variety of contexts.

The relationship between understanding concepts and being proficient with procedures is further developed in the examples of the Probes that follow. Both conceptual understanding and procedural flexibility are important goals that complement each other in developing strong

**Table 1.1** Procedural versus Conceptual Understanding

| Procedural Knowledge | Accompanying Conceptual Understanding | Examples |
|---|---|---|
| Learn and apply a series of steps | • Explain why the steps make sense mathematically<br>• Use reasoning to rebuild the steps if needed<br>• Make connections between alternative steps that could be used to find the solution<br>• Describe the parts of a formula and relate the parts to various models/representation of situations involving use of the formula | When asked to determine the solution to a quadratic equation, the student chooses the most efficient solution method given the format of the equation and the context involved and can explain why a particular solution method was used.<br><br>Recognizes the part of the formula that represents the area of the base for any 3-D solid. |
| Find a solution | • Show flexibility in representing and categorizing mathematical situations<br>• Justify whether the answer makes sense (example: reasoning about the size of an unknown number within an equation)<br>• Troubleshoot a mistake<br>• Represent thinking with symbols, models, and/or diagrams | Without actually calculating, reasons that $-\dfrac{15x}{7} \div \dfrac{3}{5}$ is about $-4x$ since it is approximately $-2x$ divided by $\dfrac{1}{2}$.<br><br>Can categorize functions represented in various forms. |
| Apply a rule | • Explain why the rule makes sense mathematically | Explains how the determinant is used to determine whether solutions to quadratic equations are real.<br><br>Can show or explain why the exponents are added (or subtracted) when simplifying multiplicative expressions with exponents. |

mathematical abilities. Each is necessary and only together do they become sufficient.

The following examples of Probes will further distinguish conceptual and procedural understandings.

## Example 1: Equation of the Function Probe

In the Equation of the Function Probe (see Figure 1.3), students with conceptual and procedural understanding pay attention to the key features of the graph in relationship to the equation. Students with conceptual understanding know that although the scale on the $x$- and $y$-axes is unknown, the graph of the function shows a positive $y$-intercept and increasing positive rate of change. This information can be determined from each of the equations. More information about this Probe can be found on pages 120–125.

Figure 1.3   Equation of the Function

### Equation of the Function

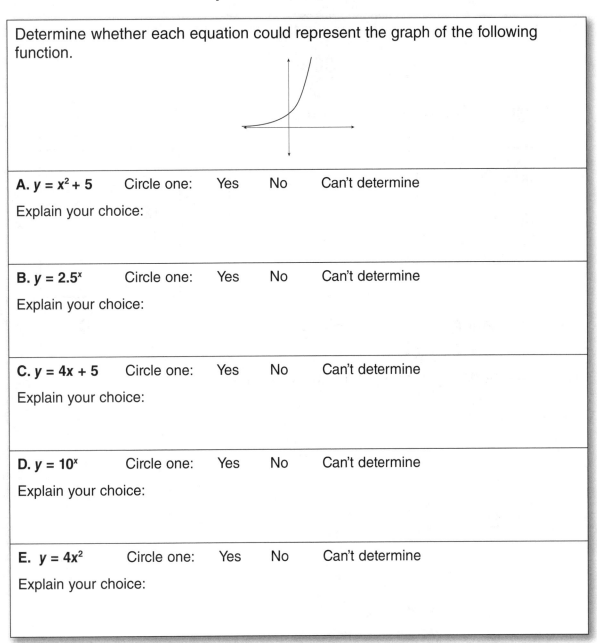

Determine whether each equation could represent the graph of the following function.

**A. $y = x^2 + 5$**      Circle one:      Yes      No      Can't determine

Explain your choice:

**B. $y = 2.5^x$**      Circle one:      Yes      No      Can't determine

Explain your choice:

**C. $y = 4x + 5$**      Circle one:      Yes      No      Can't determine

Explain your choice:

**D. $y = 10^x$**      Circle one:      Yes      No      Can't determine

Explain your choice:

**E. $y = 4x^2$**      Circle one:      Yes      No      Can't determine

Explain your choice:

## Example 2: Solving for a Variable Probe

In the Solving for a Variable Probe (see Figure 1.4), students with conceptual understanding can reason about the size of the answer without having to do the actual calculations because they understand the relationship between the numbers, symbols, and operations within the equation. More information about this Probe can be found on pages 66–72.

---

**Figure 1.4**   Solving for a Variable

### Solving for a Variable

Students were asked to solve for $x$ in the following equation.

$$36 = \frac{12}{x}$$

Three students have each solved the problem differently.

| Student **A** | Student **B** | Student **C** |
|---|---|---|
| $36 = \dfrac{12}{x}$ | $36 = \dfrac{12}{x}$ | $36 = \dfrac{12}{x}$ |
| $12\,(36) = x$ | $\dfrac{36}{12} = x$ | $\dfrac{12}{36} = x$ |
| $x = 432$ | $x = 3$ | $x = \dfrac{1}{3}$ |

Circle the student you think correctly solved for $x$.

Explain your choice:

## Example 3: Geometry Formulas Card Sort Probe

In the Geometry Formulas Card Sort Probe (see Figure 1.5), students with conceptual and procedural understanding pay attention to the key features of a formula in order to reason about the connections between and among various formulas. They are also able to describe comparisons and/ or differences among formulas grouped together. More information about this Probe can be found on pages 165–172.

**Figure 1.5**   Geometry Formulas Card Sort

## Geometry Formulas Card Sort

| Area | Volume | G. $\dfrac{x_2 + x_1}{2}, \dfrac{y_2 + y_1}{2}$ | H. $\dfrac{bh}{2}$ |
|---|---|---|---|
| Distance | Other | I. $\sqrt{(x_2 - x_1)^2 + (y_2 - y_1)^2}$ | J. $\dfrac{(b_1 + b_2)h}{2}$ |
| A. $Bh$ | B. $\dfrac{y_2 - y_1}{x_2 - x_1}$ | K. $2\pi r$ | L. $s^2$ |
| C. $\dfrac{4\pi r^3}{3}$ | D. $leg^2 + leg^2 = hyp^2$ | M. $\dfrac{Bh}{3}$ | N. $\pi r^2$ |
| E. $lw$ | F. $2l + 2w$ | | |

# UNCOVERING STUDENT UNDERSTANDING: USE A PROBE TO UNCOVER UNDERSTANDINGS AND AREAS OF DIFFICULTIES

Misunderstandings are likely to develop as a normal part of learning mathematics. These misunderstandings can be classified as conceptual misunderstandings, overgeneralizations, preconceptions, and partial conceptions. These are summarized in Figure 1.6, and each is described in more detail next.

**Figure 1.6**  Mathematics Assessment Probes

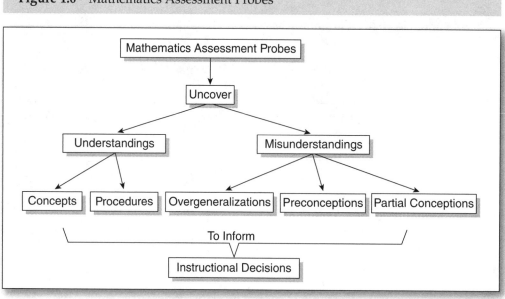

*Source:* Adapted from Rose, Minton, and Arline (2007).

In *Hispanic and Anglo Students' Misconceptions in Mathematics,* Jose Mestre (1989) summarizes cognitive research as follows: Students do not come to the classroom as "blank slates" (Resnick, 1983). Instead, they come with theories constructed from their everyday experiences. They have actively constructed these theories, an activity crucial to all successful learning. Some of the theories that students use to make sense of the world are, however, incomplete half-truths (Mestre, 1989). They are misconceptions.

Misconceptions are a problem for two reasons. First, when students use them to interpret new experiences, misconceptions interfere with learning. Second, because they have actively constructed them, students are emotionally and intellectually attached to their misconceptions. Even when students recognize that their misconceptions can harm their learning, they are reluctant to let them go. Given this, it is critical that high school teachers uncover and address their students' misconceptions as soon as possible.

For the purposes of this book, misconceptions will be categorized as *overgeneralizations, partial conceptions,* and *conceptual misunderstandings.* The following brief summary describes each of these categories of misconception:

- *Overgeneralizations:* Information extended or applied to another context in an inappropriate way. Overgeneralizations also include vernacular issues related to differences between the everyday meaning of words and their mathematical meaning.
- *Partial Conception:* Hybrids of correct and incorrect ideas. This may result from difficulty generalizing or connecting concepts or distinguishing between two concepts.
- *Conceptual Misunderstandings:* Content students "learned" in school but that has been misinterpreted and internalized: These misunderstandings often go unnoticed by the teacher. Students often make their own meaning out of what is taught. (Adapted from Keeley, 2012)

Table 1.2 provides an example from each of the above categories. The examples provided are from the progressions for the Common Core State Standards in Mathematics written by the Common Core Standards Writing Team (2012, 2013a, 2013b, 2013c).

**Table 1.2**   Misconceptions: Categories and Examples

| *Misconception Category* | *Example* |
|---|---|
| **Overgeneralizations:** Information extended or applied to another context in an inappropriate way | "Students sometimes interpret the parentheses in function notation as indicating multiplication. Because they might have seen numerical expressions like 3(4), meaning 3 times 4, students can interpret $f(x)$ as $f$ times $x$. This can lead to false generalizations of the distributive property, such as replacing $f(x + 3)$ with $f(x) + f(3)$." "Students can get confused about the effect of transformations on the input variable, because the effect on the graph appears to be the opposite to the transformation on the variable." |
| **Partial Conception:** Hybrids of correct and incorrect ideas. This may result from difficulty generalizing or connecting concepts or distinguishing between two concepts. | "The traditional emphasis on simplification as an automatic procedure might lead students to automatically convert the second two forms to the first, before considering which form is most useful in a given context. This can lead to time consuming detours in algebraic work, such as solving $(x + 1)(x - 3) = 0$ by first expanding and then applying the quadratic formula." |

*(Continued)*

(Continued)

| Misconception Category | Example |
|---|---|
| | "The development of polynomials and rational expressions in high school parallels the development of numbers in elementary school. In elementary school students might initially see expressions like 8+ 3 and 11, or $\frac{3}{4}$ and 0.75, as fundamentally different: 8 + 3 might be seen as describing a calculation and 11 is its answer; $\frac{3}{4}$ is a fraction and 75 is a decimal. Gradually they come to see numbers as forming a unified system, the number system, represented by points on the number line, and these different expressions are different ways of naming an underlying thing, a number. A similar evolution takes place in algebra. At first algebraic expressions are simply numbers in which one or more letters are used to stand for a number which is either unspecified or unknown. Students learn to use the properties of operations to write expressions in different but equivalent forms. At some point they see equivalent expressions, particularly polynomial and rational expressions, as naming some underlying thing." |
| **Conceptual Misunderstandings:** Content that students "learned" in school but that has been misinterpreted and internalized | "Students must see that one of the most common misinterpretations of correlation is to think of it as a synonym for causation. A high correlation between two variables (suggesting a statistical association between the two) does *not* imply that one causes the other." |

*Examples Source:* Common Core Standards Writing Team (2012, 2103a, 2103c, 2013c).

Some misunderstandings do not fall distinctly into one category but can be characterized in more than one way. For example, the conceptual misunderstanding of the base of a triangle can also be considered an over-generalization. In addition, some misconceptions are more deeply rooted and difficult to change than others. It is important to make the distinction between what we might call a silly mistake and a more fundamental one that may be the product of a deep-rooted misunderstanding. In her guest editorial "Misunderstanding Misconceptions," Page Keeley describes various practitioner misunderstandings related to using the science Probes in the National Science Teachers Association's *Uncovering Student Ideas in*

*Science* series (Keeley, 2012, pp. 12–15). Both in our work with Page and with mathematics educators using the *Uncovering Student Thinking in Mathematics* resources, we have encountered many similar misunderstandings among teachers:

- *All misconceptions are the same.* The word *misconception* is frequently used to describe all ideas students bring to their learning that are not completely accurate. In contrast, researchers often use labels such as *alternative frameworks, naive ideas, phenomenological primitives, children's ideas,* and so on to imply that these ideas are not completely "wrong" in a student's commonsense world.

- *Misconceptions are a bad thing.* The word *misconception* seems to have a pejorative connotation to most practitioners. According to constructivist theory, when new ideas are encountered, they are accepted, rejected, or modified to fit existing conceptions. It is the cognitive dissonance students experience when they realize an existing mental model no longer works for them that makes students willing to give up a preexisting idea in favor of a scientific one. Having ideas to work from, even if they are not completely accurate, leads to deeper understanding when students engage in a conceptual-change process (Watson & Konicek, 1990).

- *All misconceptions are major barriers to learning.* Just as some learning standards have more weight in promoting conceptual learning than others, the same is true of misconceptions. For example, a student may have a misconception for only one type of modeling situation but can make great strides in learning to model and represent operations for other situations. (Adapted from Keeley, 2012)

To teach in a way that avoids creating any misconceptions is not possible, and we have to accept that students will make some incorrect generalizations that will remain hidden unless the teacher makes specific efforts to uncover them (Askew & Wiliam, 1995). Our job as educators is to minimize the chances of students' harboring misconceptions by knowing the potential difficulties students are likely to encounter, using assessments to elicit misconceptions, and implementing instruction designed to build new and accurate mathematical ideas.

The primary purpose of the Probes is to elicit understandings and areas of difficulties related to specific mathematical ideas. In addition to these content-specific related targets, the Probes also elicit skills and processes related to the Standards for Mathematical Practices, especially those related to use of reasoning and explanation. If you are unfamiliar with the Standards for Mathematical Practices or would like a refresher, descriptions of them can be found in Appendix A.

## WHAT IS THE STRUCTURE OF A PROBE?

The Probes are designed to include two levels of response, one for elicitation of common understandings and misunderstandings and the other for the elaboration of individual student thinking. Each of the levels is described in more detail next.

## Level 1: Answer Response

Since the elicitation level is designed to uncover common understandings and misunderstandings, a structured format using stems, correct answers, and distractors is used to narrow ideas found in the related research. The formats typically fall into one of three categories, shown in Figures 1.7 though 1.9.

### Selected Response Probes

- Two or more items are provided, each with one stem (or prompt), one correct answer, and one or more distractors; or
- Two or more separate problems or statements are provided, each with an answer choice needing to be justified

**Figure 1.7**   Logarithms Probe

## Logarithms

| Given the following information, which of the following are true? |
|---|
| $$\log_{10} y = x \quad \text{and} \quad x < 0$$ |
| Explain your reasoning on each choice. |

| **A.** $y < 0$ | Circle one: | Sometimes | Always | Never |
|---|---|---|---|---|
| Explain your choice: | | | | |

| **B.** $y = 0$ | Circle one: | Sometimes | Always | Never |
|---|---|---|---|---|
| Explain your choice: | | | | |

| **C.** $0 < y < 1$ | Circle one: | Sometimes | Always | Never |
|---|---|---|---|---|
| Explain your choice: | | | | |

| **D.** $y > 10$ | Circle one: | Sometimes | Always | Never |
|---|---|---|---|---|
| Explain your choice: | | | | |

### Math Talk Probe

- Two or more statements are provided and students choose the statement they agree with. This format is adapted from *Concept Cartoons in Science Education,* created by Stuart Naylor and Brenda Keogh (2000) for probing student ideas in science.

**Figure 1.8**    Modeling With Linear Graphs Probe

## Modeling With Linear Graphs

The following graph shows data a group of students found on ice cream sales in dollars (*y* values) versus temperature in °C (*x* values). They drew a best-fit line and found the equation of the line to be $y = 19.5x + 100$. When the same data were entered into a graphing calculator and a regression model found, the equation was $y = 30x - 159.5$. Why is the best-fit equation so different from the regression model?

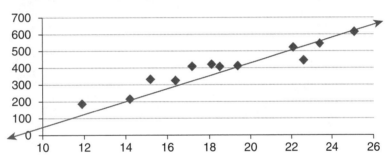

I think it is different because they did not find the best-fit line.

**McKayla**

I think it is different because their graph does not show all of the *x* intervals.

**Olivia**

I think it is different because they probably didn't put the data into the calculator accurately.

**Dylan**

Who do you agree with and why?

### *Examples and Nonexamples Probes*

- Several examples and nonexamples are given, and students are asked to sort the items into the correct piles or select yes or no and justify their choice.

---

**Figure 1.9** Matrix Equations Probe

## Matrix Equations

Given the following System of Equations, decide whether each matrix equation accurately represents the system.

$$3x + 2y = 14 \qquad y - 4x = -6$$

| | | |
|---|---|---|
| A. $\begin{bmatrix} 3 & 1 \\ 2 & -4 \end{bmatrix} \cdot \begin{bmatrix} x \\ y \end{bmatrix} = \begin{bmatrix} 14 \\ -6 \end{bmatrix}$ | Circle one: | Yes    No |
| Explain your choice: | | |
| B. $\begin{bmatrix} 3 & 2 \\ 1 & -4 \end{bmatrix} \cdot \begin{bmatrix} x \\ y \end{bmatrix} = \begin{bmatrix} 14 \\ -6 \end{bmatrix}$ | Circle one: | Yes    No |
| Explain your choice: | | |
| C. $\begin{bmatrix} 3 & 2 \\ -4 & 1 \end{bmatrix} \cdot \begin{bmatrix} x \\ y \end{bmatrix} = \begin{bmatrix} 14 \\ -6 \end{bmatrix}$ | Circle one: | Yes    No |
| Explain your choice: | | |
| D. $\begin{bmatrix} 3x & 1y \\ 2x & -4y \end{bmatrix} \cdot \begin{bmatrix} x \\ y \end{bmatrix} = \begin{bmatrix} 14 \\ -6 \end{bmatrix}$ | Circle one: | Yes    No |
| Explain your choice: | | |
| E. $\begin{bmatrix} 2 & 3 \\ 1 & -4 \end{bmatrix} \cdot \begin{bmatrix} x \\ y \end{bmatrix} = \begin{bmatrix} 14 \\ -6 \end{bmatrix}$ | Circle one: | Yes    No |
| Explain your choice: | | |

### Level 2: Explanation of Response Choice

The second level of each of the Probes is designed so students can elaborate on the reasoning they used to respond to the Level 1 elicitation question. Mathematics teachers gain a wealth of information by delving into the thinking behind students' answers, not just when answers are wrong but also when they are correct. Although the Level 1 answers and distractors are designed to target common understandings and misunderstandings, the elaboration level allows educators to look more deeply at student thinking. Often a student chooses a specific response, correct or incorrect, for a typical reason. Also, there are many different ways to approach a problem correctly; therefore, the elaboration level allows educators to look for patterns in thinking and in methods used. Chapter 7 delves deeper into expectations for this elaboration and its relationship to the Common Core Mathematical Practices.

## QUEST CYCLE: STRUCTURE OF THE SUPPORTING TEACHER NOTES

The Teacher Notes, included with each Probe, have been designed to help you prepare for a QUEST Cycle. The first two components of the cycle, *determining the key mathematical understandings* and *uncovering student understandings and areas of difficulties,* have been described more fully earlier. We use the description of the Teacher Notes to provide more details about the remaining components of the cycle.

### Questions to Consider About the Key Mathematical Concepts

This section of the Teacher Notes helps to focus a teacher on the key conceptual and procedural mathematics addressed by the particular Probe and gives information about alignment to Common Core standards to a particular course. Figure 1.10 shows an example from this section of the Transformation of Functions Teacher Notes.

**Figure 1.10**  Questions to Consider About the Key Mathematical Concepts

> When working with functions, do students understand how algebraic representations describe graphical transformations? To what extent do they
>
> - make sense of various forms of algebraic representations and correctly relate it to a graphical transformation?
> - reason about the algebraic and graphical connections?
> - describe graphical effects of various algebraic transformations?
>
> *(Continued)*

(Continued)

## Common Core Connection
## (CCSS.Math.Content.HSF-BF.B.3)

**Grade:** High School

**Domain:** Functions

**Clusters:**

**Build new functions from existing functions.**

B.3 Identify the effect on the graph of replacing $f(x)$ by $f(x) + k$, $k\,f(x)$, $f(kx)$, and $f(x + k)$ for specific values of $k$ (both positive and negative); find the value of $k$ given the graphs. Experiment with cases and illustrate an explanation of the effects on the graph using technology. Include recognizing even and odd functions from their graphs and algebraic expressions for them.

# *U*ncovering Student Understanding About the Key Concepts

This section of the Teacher Notes (Figure 1.11) breaks down the concepts and ideas described in the "Questioning" section into specific understandings and areas of difficulty targeted by the Probe.

**Figure 1.11**   Uncovering Student Understanding About the Key Concepts

Using the Transformation of Functions Probe can provide the following information about how the students are thinking about algebraic and graphical transformations.

*Do they*

- recognize a horizontal or vertical translation and/or stretch?

OR

- correctly apply the direction of a translation using the opposite sign of the number connected with the *x* value and the same sign of the number that is connected with the *y* value?

OR

- understand that multiplying by a negative number "flips" the graph?

OR

*Do they*

- not recognize the placement of the numbers as a clue as to the type of translation?

- apply an incorrect direction to the translation?

- see the negative as only part of the number that will stretch the graph?

# *E*xploring Excerpts From Educational Resources and Related Research

This section of the Teacher Notes (Figure 1.12) includes excerpts from cognitive research related to the common areas of difficulty targeted by the Probe. The excerpts are meant to provide some background from the research base behind the development of the Probe. The references provide an opportunity for you to seek additional information when needed. This research base is an important component in the Probe development process. More information on the origin of the Probe development process can be found in Appendix B.

**Figure 1.12** Exploring Excerpts From Educational Resources and Related Research

Areas of consideration:

The concept of function transformations is a central theme from algebra through calculus, yet it is one that many students fail to internalize. (Poetzel, Muskin, Munroe, & Russell, 2012, p. 103)

Students may find the effect of adding a constant to the input variable to be counterintuitive, because the effect on the graph appears to be the opposite to the transformation on the variable, e.g., the graph of $y = f(x + 2)$ is a horizontal translation of the graph of $y = f(x) - 2$ units along the $x$-axis rather than in the opposite direction. (Common Core Standards Writing Team, 2013b)

When a problem involves a function which can be the result of the application of a set of transformations on a basic function, students are generally able to identify some of the transformations that have been applied. Students who had difficulties with this type of tasks found troublesome to associate a function represented graphically with its corresponding analytical representation. They showed a tendency to use memorized facts or to make a table of data in order to succeed in these tasks. . . . A smaller group of students showed a tendency to generalize the conservation of distance property, which is valid for rigid transformations, to non-rigid transformations, demonstrating that they apply actions or processes to the graph of the function as if it was a rigid object, with no reflection on what the result of those actions would be for each particular point on the domain of the function. . . . In questions related to rigid transformations, students had more difficulties recognizing a horizontal translation than a vertical translation. This seems to be due to the fact that students memorize the rules for transformations and their corresponding effect on the function. When remembering this information students often associate the incorrect direction to the translation. (Alatorre, Cortina, Sáiz, & Méndez, 2006, pp. 26–27)

# *S*urveying the Prompts and Selected Responses in the Probe

This section of the Teacher Notes (Figure 1.13) includes information about the prompt, selected response/answer(s), and the distractors. Sample student responses are given for a selected number of elicited understandings and misunderstandings. This initial preparation will help expedite the analysis process once you administer the Probe to students.

**Figure 1.13**  Surveying the Prompts and Selected Responses in the Probe

The Probe consists of four separate selected response items. The prompts and selected responses are designed to elicit understandings and common difficulties as described below:

| If a student chooses | It is likely that the student |
|---|---|
| 1a, 2b, 3b, 4d (correct responses) | • recognizes graphical transformations based on algebraic representations. [See Sample Student Response 1]<br><br>*Look for indication of the student's understanding in the written explanations of how the student got the answer.* |
| Various other response patterns | • fails to recognize various features of algebraic representations that show graphical transformation. Many times this has to do with the error in direction of a translation (Questions 3 and 4) or how a function is vertically or horizontally stretched (Question 2). [See Sample Student Responses 2, 3, 4, and 5] |

# *T*eaching Implications and Considerations

Being aware of student difficulties and their sources is important, but acting on that information to design and provide instruction that will diminish those difficulties is even more important. The information in this section of the Teacher Notes (Figure 1.14) is broken into two categories: (1) ideas for eliciting more information from students about their understanding and difficulties and (2) ideas for planning instruction in response to what you learned from the results of administering the Probe. Although these ideas are included in the Teacher Notes, we strongly encourage you to pursue additional research-based teaching implications.

**Figure 1.14**  Teaching Implications and Considerations

Ideas for eliciting more information from students about their understanding and difficulties:

- What is the parent function? What does the parent function look like? What are some key features of the parent function?
- What does each term tell you about the graph?
- We need to be careful about the signs of the numbers. What do the different signs tell you?
- Can you graph this and explain the transformation? Can you show me how the graph correlates to the equation (algebraic representation)?

Ideas for planning instruction in response to what you learned from the results of administering the Probe:

- Use technology to introduce transformations. Explore individual transformations from a parent function to allow students to understand one transformation at a time. Let them "see" what the numbers in the algebraic representation "do" to the graph.
- When working with equations, show students that the number that correlates with a vertical translation can be placed with the $y$ variable so that they see the opposite number is taken just like the number with the $x$ variable (write $y = -2(x - 4)^2 - 7$ as $y + 7 = -2(x - 4)^2$). Students can see that by moving the 7 to the other side of the equation, the opposite sign is already being accounted for.
- Allow students to explore various types of functions (linear, quadratic, square root, absolute value, cubic, piecewise, trigonometric, etc.). This allows students to see how the transformation "rules" apply to all functions.
- Integrate the study of transformations throughout the study of functions, starting with linear and moving to higher order functions.

Included in the Teaching section of the Teacher Notes are sample student responses; examples of these are shown in Figure 1.15.

**Figure 1.15**   Sample Student Responses to Transformation of Functions

**Responses That Suggest Understanding**

*Sample Student Response 1*

Probe Item 1: Student chose a. Because of the leading negative, the graph is reflected over the $x$-axis (flipped).

Probe Item 2: Student chose b. The number in front of the parenthesis is greater than 1; this graph grows faster than the parent function and therefore is stretched vertically.

Probe Item 3: Student chose b. The −4 is what moves the graph horizontally as it is with the $x$ value. It moves in the opposite direction and therefore in the positive direction (right) 4 units.

Probe Item 4: Student chose d. The −7 is what moves the graph vertically. It was originally with the $y$ value as a +7, and we have already taken the opposite value by moving it to the right side; therefore, it would move it up 7 units.

*(Continued)*

(Continued)

**Responses That Suggest Difficulty**

*Sample Student Response 2*

Probe Item 1: Student chose d. Without graphing this we cannot tell if it is reflected or not. Put it into a graphing calculator to see.

*Sample Student Response 3*

Probe Item 2: Student chose d. The 2 makes it more narrow, I think, but I am not sure if it stretches it or not.

*Sample Student Response 4*

Probe Item 3: Student chose a. The neg 4 moves it left or right and neg is to the left, so left 4 units would be the right answer.

*Sample Student Response 5*

Probe Item 4: Student chose c. The 7 moves the graph up or down, and we need to take the opposite sign. This would mean in the positive direction (up) 7 units.

### Variations

For some Probes, adaptations and variations are provided and can be found following the Teacher Notes and sample student responses to the Probe. A variation of a Probe provides an alternative structure (selected response, multiple selections, opposing views, or examples/nonexamples) for the question within the same course. In contrast, an adaptation to a Probe is similar in content to the original, but the level of mathematics is changed for a different level of mathematics content.

### Action Research Reflection Template

A Reflection Template is included in Appendix C. The Reflection Template provides a structured approach to working through the QUEST Cycle with a Probe. The components of the template are described in Figure 1.16.

## BEGINNING TO USE THE PROBES

Now that you have a background on the design of the Probes, the accompanying Teacher Notes, and the QUEST Cycle, it is time to think about how to get started using the Probes with your students.

**Figure 1.16**    Reflection Template

### Questions to Consider About the Key Mathematical Concepts

What is the concept you wish to target? Is the concept at course level or is it a prerequisite?

### Uncovering Student Understanding About the Key Concepts

How will you collect information from students (e.g., paper-pencil, interview, student response system)? What form will you use (e.g., one-page Probe, card sort)? Are there adaptations you plan to make? Review the summary of typical student responses.

### Exploring Excerpts From Educational Resources and Related Research

Review the quotes from research about common difficulties related to the Probe. What do you predict to be common understandings and/or misunderstandings for your students?

### Surveying the Prompts and Selected Responses in the Probe

Sort by selected responses and then re-sort by trends in thinking. What common understandings/misunderstandings did the Probe elicit? How do these elicited understandings/misunderstandings compare to those listed in the Teacher Notes?

### Teaching Implications and Considerations

Review the bulleted list and decide how you will take action. What actions did you take? How did you assess the impact of those actions? What are your next steps?

*Choosing a Probe:* Determining which Probe to use depends on a number of factors, including time of year, alignment to curriculum, and range of abilities within your classroom. We recommend not only that you spend some time reviewing the Probes for your courses first but also that you make note of additional Probes that may be appropriate for your students.

*Deciding How to Administer a Probe:* Depending on your purpose, Probes can be given to one student or to all students in your classroom. You may wish to give a Probe to only one student (or several) if you notice the student or group is struggling with a related concept. By giving a Probe to all students, you can gain a sense of patterns of understanding and difficulty in order to target instruction. Although all probes can be given as a written explanation, we encourage you to use the probes as interview prompts in order to probe their thinking even further. Using the Probes in interviews is described in more detail in Chapter 7.

*Talking With Students About Probes:* Probes are not meant to be graded! We have found that students "buy into" the diagnostic nature of the Probes, especially if the process is shared explicitly with them. Talk to your students about the importance of explaining their thinking in mathematics and why you will ask additional questions to understand more about their thinking.

When giving a Probe, be sure to read through the directions, repeating them as necessary. Do not try to correct students on the spot; instead, ask additional probing questions to determine whether the additional questions prompt the student to think differently. If not, do not stop to try to teach the students "in the moment." Instead, take in the information and think about the next appropriate instructional steps. If students are having difficulty, reassure them that you will be working with them to learn more about the content in the Probe.

## HOW TO NAVIGATE THE BOOK

This chapter provided the background information needed to begin to dig into the Probes and think about how you will use them with your students. The next five chapters include twenty-five sets of Probes and accompanying Teacher Notes, and the final chapter includes additional considerations for using the Probes.

### Chapters 2 Through 6: The Probes

Table 1.3 provides an at-a-glance look of the targeted question and related domain of the content of the twenty-five Probes.

The beginning of each Probe chapter (Chapters 2–6) includes background on the development of the Probes to align with the relevant Common Core domain and standards and a summary chart to guide your review and selection of Probes and variations to use with your students.

### Chapter 7: Additional Considerations

The QUEST Cycle components are explained in detail within this chapter as well as for each specific Probe through the accompanying Teacher Notes. In addition to these ideas that are specific to the Probe are instructional considerations that cut across the Probes. Such considerations include ways to use the Probes over time to promote mathematical discussions, support and assess students' ability to provide justification, and promote conceptual change.

**Table 1.3** Mathematics Assessment Probes

| Probe Name | Common Core Domain and Cluster | Probe-Related Question |
|---|---|---|
| Complex Numbers (p. 30) | Number and Quantity: The Real Number System | Do students understand the properties of complex numbers? |
| Rational Exponents (p. 35) | Number and Quantity: The Real Number System | Can students use the properties of exponents and convert between rational exponents and radicals to simplify expressions? |
| Operating With Matrices (p. 43) | Number and Quantity: Vector and Matrix Quantities | Can students correctly multiply matrices and recognize when matrix multiplication cannot be performed because of inappropriate matrix dimensions? |
| Equivalent Expressions (p. 53) | Algebra: Seeing Structure in Expressions and Arithmetic With Polynomials and Rational Expressions | Can students correctly identify equivalent expressions involving exponents? |
| Simplifying Rational Expressions (p. 61) | Algebra: Arithmetic With Polynomials and Rational Expressions | Can students use algebraic techniques, including factoring, to correctly simplify rational expressions? |
| Solving for a Variable (p. 66) | Algebra: Reasoning With Equations and Inequalities | Can students correctly reason about solving equations when the variable is in the denominator? |
| Solving Quadratic Equations (p. 73) | Algebra: Reasoning With Equations and Inequalities | When analyzing quadratic equations, can students determine when an equation has real solutions (roots, zeros, $x$-intercepts)? |
| Systems of Linear Equations (p. 78) | Algebra: Reasoning With Equations and Inequalities | Can students analyze pairs of systems of equations in order to determine similarities and differences among their solution sets? |
| Matrix Equations (p. 83) | Algebra: Reasoning With Equations and Inequalities | Can students represent a system of linear equations as a matrix equation? |
| Jogging: Graphical Representation (p. 90) | Functions: Interpreting Functions | When interpreting graphs and verbal descriptions, do students understand and use key descriptive features instead of interpreting graphs as literal pictures? |
| Interpreting Functions (p. 96) | Functions: Interpreting Functions | When interpreting graphical representations of functions, do students recognize domain intervals where a function is increasing, decreasing, or constant? |

*(Continued)*

(Continued)

| Probe Name | Common Core Domain and Cluster | Probe-Related Question |
|---|---|---|
| Transformation of Functions (p. 101) | Functions: Building Functions | When working with functions, do students understand how algebraic representations describe graphical transformations? |
| Circular Measurement (p. 107) | Functions: Trigonometric Functions | When solving problems with circular measurements, can students accurately determine an estimate measure of an arc drawn in a circle? |
| Direct and Inverse Variation (p. 112) | Functions: Linear, Quadratic, and Exponential Functions  Algebra: Creating Equations | Can students distinguish between examples and nonexamples of direct and inverse relationships? |
| Equation of the Function (p. 120) | Functions: Linear, Quadratic, and Exponential Functions | When given a graph of an exponential function without labeled intervals, can students determine possible algebraic representations of the graph? |
| Logarithms (p. 126) | Functions: Linear, Quadratic, and Exponential Functions | When analyzing logarithms, do students understand how to evaluate a logarithm by first expressing it as an exponential equation? |
| Properties of Angles (p. 135) | Geometry: Congruence | When solving problems involving relationships between interior and exterior angles of a triangle, can students use characteristics and properties to compare angle measures? |
| Is It a Parallelogram? (p. 141) | Geometry: Congruence | Can students use properties of parallelograms to prove whether a figure is a parallelogram? |
| Names of the Shape (p. 147) | Geometry: Geometric Measurement and Dimension | When working with three-dimensional figures, can students correctly identify them? |
| Circles and Angles (p. 152) | Geometry: Circles | When solving problems with circles, can students identify and use relationships among central and inscribed angles to solve measurement problems? |
| Trigonometric Ratios (p. 159) | Geometry: Similarity, Right Triangles, and Trigonometry | When solving for unknown side lengths or angle measures in right triangles, can students recognize correct trigonometric ratios to use? |
| Geometry Formulas Card Sort (p. 165) | Geometry: Similarity, Right Triangles, and Trigonometry and Geometric Measurement and Dimension | Do students recognize what various geometric formulas are used for? |

| Probe Name | Common Core Domain and Cluster | Probe-Related Question |
|---|---|---|
| Modeling With Linear Graphs (p. 176) | Statistics and Probability: Interpreting Categorical and Quantitative Data | When analyzing linear data graphically, can students interpret the rate of change (slope) and y-intercept when the graph does not start at the origin? |
| Comparing Data in Box Plots (p. 182) | Statistics and Probability: Interpreting Categorical and Quantitative Data | When working with box plots, can students analyze and compare data sets without a given scale? |
| Probability (p. 190) | Statistics and Probability: Conditional Probability and the Rules of Probability | When working with probability problems, do students recognize when to apply addition or multiplication rules? |

We recommend that you scan the contents of Chapter 7 before beginning to use Probes but that you not try to "do it all" the first time out. After using the Probes, return to Chapter 7 to pinpoint one or two considerations to implement and try out those ideas before returning to consider implementing additional idea s.

## FINAL CHAPTER 1 THOUGHTS

We hope these Probes will support you in your work in trying to uncover your students' thinking and understanding and will inspire you to explore ways to respond to their strengths and difficulties in order to move students' learning forward.

# 2

# Number and Quantity Probes

The content of the Probes in this chapter aligns with the standards for high school but is often taught in different courses across districts. The Probes and their variations are also relevant beyond the aligned course level for students in more advanced courses who have not yet met particular standards from previous courses as well as for students who have already met the standards in the current course.

We developed these Probes to address this critical area of focus for high school students, described in the standards (Council of Chief State School Officers [CCSSO], 2010) as follows:

- Rewrite expressions involving radicals and rational exponents using the properties of exponents.
- Know there is a complex number $i$ such that $i^2 = -1$, and every complex number has the form $a + bi$ with $a$ and $b$ real.
- Use the relation $i^2 = -1$ and the commutative, associative, and distributive properties to add, subtract, and multiply complex numbers.
- Find the conjugate of a complex number; use conjugates to find moduli and quotients of complex numbers.
- Multiply matrices by scalars to produce new matrices (e.g., as when all of the payoffs in a game are doubled).
- Add, subtract, and multiply matrices of appropriate dimensions.
- Understand that, unlike multiplication of numbers, matrix multiplication for square matrices is not a commutative operation but still satisfies the associative and distributive properties.

- Understand that the zero and identity matrices play a role in matrix addition and multiplication similar to the role of 0 and 1 in the real numbers. The determinant of a square matrix is nonzero if and only if the matrix has a multiplicative inverse.

The standards and their related questions, as well as the Probes associated with them, are shown in Table 2.1.

> The content of the Probes in this chapter aligns with the standards for high school but is often taught in different courses across districts. The Probes and their variations are also relevant beyond the aligned course level for students in more advanced courses who have not yet met particular standards from previous courses as well as for students who have already met the standards in the current course.

**Table 2.1** Number and Quantity Probes

| Common Core Mathematical Content | Related Question | Probe Name |
|---|---|---|
| Know there is a complex number $i$ such that $i^2 = -1$, and every complex number has the form $a + bi$ with $a$ and $b$ real.<br><br>*CCSS.Math.Content.HSN-CN.A.1*<br><br>Use the relation $i^2 = -1$ and the commutative, associative, and distributive properties to add, subtract, and multiply complex numbers.<br><br>*CCSS.Math.Content.HSN-CN.A.2* | Do students understand the properties of complex numbers? | Complex Numbers (p. 30) |
| Rewrite expressions involving radicals and rational exponents using the properties of exponents.<br><br>*CCSS.Math.Content.HSN-RN.A.2* | Can students use the properties of exponents and convert between rational exponents and radicals to simplify expressions? | Rational Exponents (p. 35)<br><br>Variation: Rational Exponents (p. 40)<br><br>Variation: Understanding Radicals (p. 41) |
| Add, subtract, and multiply matrices of appropriate dimensions.<br><br>*CCSS.Math.Content.HSN-VM.C.8* | Can students correctly multiply matrices and recognize when matrix multiplication cannot be performed because of inappropriate matrix dimensions? | Operating With Matrices (p. 43)<br><br>Variation: Matrices (p. 48) |

Take a look at the variations that are available with some of the Probes in this chapter. All of these variations address number system ideas but may extend the idea or offer a different structure for administering them. When available, variation Probes follow the Teacher Notes and associated reproducibles for the related original Probe.

## Complex Numbers

Choose if each statement is true or false and justify your choice.

| Circle the correct answer. | Justify your choice. |
|---|---|
| **1.**<br><br>*i* **to an odd power is always equal to** $\sqrt{-1}$ **.**<br><br>a. True<br><br>b. False | |
| **2.**<br><br>**(*a* + *bi*)(*a* − *bi*) is always a real number.**<br><br>a. True<br><br>b. False | |
| **3.**<br><br>**When adding imaginary numbers,** *i* **can be treated like a variable. For example,** 4*i* + 9*i* =13*i*.<br><br>a. True<br><br>b. False | |
| **4.**<br><br>$(i\sqrt{-x})^2$ **is always equal to** *x.*<br><br>a. True<br><br>b. False | |

## Teacher Notes: Complex Numbers

### **Q**uestions to Consider About the Key Mathematical Concepts

When working with complex numbers, do students understand the properties of operations with them? To what extent do they

- describe complex numbers as expressions of the form $a + bi$ with $i^2 = -1$?
- identify parts of a complex number that are imaginary and real?
- understand similarities and difference between operations with complex numbers and operations with other types of numbers?

---

**Common Core Connection
(CCSS.Math.Content.HSN-CN.A.1;
CCSS.Math.Content.HSN-CN.A.2)**

**Grade:** High School

**Domain:** Number and Quantity

**Clusters:**

**Perform arithmetic operations with complex numbers.**

A1. Know there is a complex number $i$ such that $i^2 = -1$, and every complex number has the form $a + bi$ with $a$ and $b$ real.

A2. Use the relation $i^2 = -1$ and the commutative, associative, and distributive properties to add, subtract, and multiply complex numbers.

---

### **U**ncovering Student Understanding About the Key Concepts

Using the Complex Numbers Probe can provide the following information about how the students are thinking about imaginary numbers and operations with complex numbers.

*Do they*

- understand $i = \sqrt{-1}$, $i^2 = -1$, $i^3 = -i$, $i^4 = 1$, $i^5 = i$, and so on?

OR

- correctly apply properties of operations with complex numbers?

OR

*Do they*

- think $i$ to an even or odd power is always equal to the same number?
- view $i$ as a variable, not as a unit with a specific value?
- overgeneralize from operations with binomials?

# *E*xploring Excerpts From Educational Resources and Related Research

Areas of consideration:

Although understanding geometric interpretations in the complex plane is not an expectation for all students in the Common Core standards, students can benefit from seeing geometric and algebraic representations developed in tandem. As a relatively new emphasis in Grades 9 through 12, students' understanding of complex numbers has not received extensive research attention. . . . The dearth of research provides an opportunity for teachers to do action research in their own classrooms. (Groth, 2013, p. 177)

Penrose (2004) notes that historically mathematicians defined $i = \sqrt{-1}$ and augmented it with two real parts, *a* and *b*, to create sums of the form $a + bi$. He explains that although the sums can be treated as a pair of numbers, acceptance of complex numbers as a new category of number is dependent on being able to conceptualize $a + bi$ as a single entity. (Conner, Rasmussen, Zandieh, & Smith, 2007, p. 2)

# *S*urveying the Prompts and Selected Responses in the Probe

The Probe consists of four true-false selected response items. The prompts and selected responses are designed to elicit understandings and common difficulties as described below:

| *If a student chooses* | *It is likely that the student* |
|---|---|
| 1. b, 2. a, 3. a, and 4. b (correct responses) | • understands *i* as $\sqrt{-1}$ and the properties of operating with complex numbers. [See Sample Student Response 1] <br><br> *Look for indication of the student's understanding in the written explanations of how the student got the answer.* |
| 1. a | • views *i* to any odd power as equal to $\sqrt{-1}$. [See Sample Student Response 2 ] |
| 2. b | • is applying ideas related to binomial multiplication $(a + bi)(a - bi) = a^2 - (bi)^2$ and not recognizing $i^2$ as $-1$. [See Sample Student Response 3] |
| 3. b | • is applying ideas related to multiplication $13i^2$ or $-13$. [See Sample Student Response 4] |
| 4. a | • views all squared numbers as positive. [See Sample Student Response 5] |

## *T*eaching Implications and Considerations

Ideas for eliciting more information from students about their understanding and difficulties:

- What is the value of $i$, $i^2$, $i^3$, and $i^4$?
- Which part of the number is imaginary and which part is real?
- If you know that $i = \sqrt{-1}$, how can you figure out what $i^2$ is ($i^2 = (\sqrt{-1})^2 = \sqrt{-1}$)? Be careful here as some students overgeneralize properties of radicals when working with negative numbers ($\sqrt{-1}\,\sqrt{-1} \neq \sqrt{(-1)(-1)}$).

Ideas for planning instruction in response to what you learned from the results of administering the Probe:

- Discuss similarities and differences between properties of operations with binomials and complex numbers.
- Provide opportunity to explore and extend the patterns associated with $i$ to various powers.
- Connect complex numbers with finding solutions to quadratics functions (using the quadratic formula). This allows connections to a discriminant that has a value less than zero.
- When working with complex number solutions to quadratic equations, develop understanding of geometric and algebraic representations concurrently. For example, when working with parabolas that don't cross the $x$-axis, have discussions on what the algebraic solutions look like. This gives students an understanding of when complex numbers are used.

### Sample Student Responses to Complex Numbers Probe

**Responses That Suggest Understanding**

*Sample Student Response 1*

Probe Item 1: Student chose b. This is false because $i$ to a power follows a pattern and doesn't start repeating again until $i^5$. That means numbers like $i^3$ and so on are not $\sqrt{-1}$.

Probe Item 3: Student chose a. This is true when adding because $i$ just stays $i$; when you multiply, though, you can substitute the $i$ sometimes with something equal.

*(Continued)*

(Continued)

**Responses That Suggest Difficulty**

*Sample Student Response 2*

Probe Item 1: Student chose a. This is true because of the pattern. It goes back and forth between certain numbers.

*Sample Student Response 3*

Probe Item 2: Student chose b. False. *i* is imaginary so not called real.

*Sample Student Response 4*

Probe Item 3: Student chose b. False. *i* is a specific number even though it is called a letter. A variable can be lots of different numbers at the same time.

*Sample Student Response 5*

Probe Item 4: Student chose a. True. Once you square it, the negative goes away.

2.2

## Rational Exponents

Simplify without using a calculator.

| Circle the correct answer. | Justify your choice. |
|---|---|
| **1.** <br><br> **Simplify** $4^{\frac{3}{2}}$ <br><br> a. 24      d. $\frac{1}{8}$ <br><br><br> b. 8      e. $\frac{1}{6}$ <br><br><br> c. 6      f. Can't be simplified | |
| **2.** <br><br> **Simplify** $(\sqrt[4]{25})^2$ <br><br> a. 200      d. $\frac{1}{25}$ <br><br><br> b. 150      e. $\frac{1}{5}$ <br><br><br> c. 5      f. Can't be simplified | |

# Teacher Notes: Rational Exponents

## Questions to Consider About the Key Mathematical Concepts

Can students use the properties of exponents and convert between rational exponents and radicals to simplify expressions? To what extent do they

- make sense of rational (fractional) exponents as an alternate way to express roots?
- reason that an expression containing a rational (fractional) power can be converted to a radical expression and vice versa to simplify it?
- describe how to use the denominator of the rational exponent as the index (root number) of the radical and the numerator as the exponent of the radicand (expression inside the radical)?

## Common Core Connection (CCSS.Math.Content.HSN-RN.A.2)

**Grade:** High School

**Domain:** Number and Quantity

**Cluster:**

**Extend the properties of exponents to rational exponents.**

A2. Rewrite expressions involving radicals and rational exponents using the properties of exponents.

## Uncovering Student Understanding About the Key Concepts

Using the Rational Exponents Probe can provide the following information about how the students are thinking about rational exponents and radicals.

*Do they*

- see the connections between radicals and rational exponents?

OR

*Do they*

- see them as separate, unrelated concepts?

*Do they*

- know how to convert between radicals and exponential expressions to make simplification easier?

OR

- transfer the properties of exponents to rational exponents?

OR

- understand what the numbers in radical notation are for (index, radicand, and power) and how they are used?

*Do they*

- try to simplify an expression based on how it is originally written?

OR

- think there are separate properties and process for each?

- associate rational exponents with rational answers?

OR

- not have a clear understanding of radical notation and often can only work with square roots?

## Exploring Excerpts From Educational Resources and Related Research

Areas of consideration:

Students are not firm with negative and fractional exponents. . . . Students have trouble with correctly simplifying. For example, Compute $16^{\left(-\frac{1}{4}\right)}$, any number of answers may be reported including $-2$ and 2 rather than correctly as $\frac{1}{2}$. (Allen, 2007, p. 4)

Rational and negative exponents are defined in textbooks by relying completely on a definition. Natural exponents refer to actions that are clear and meaningful to the student.

Definitions that have a strong familiar side and tend to be immediately clear to students are classified as "logical" definitions (i.e., logical for the learner!). Definitions that rely on features and characteristics of a concept and rely solely on these properties are classified as "lexical." Students, even in mathematics, seem to have problems with lexical definitions (Edwards, 1997; Edwards & Ward, 2004). What they develop over time is a concept-definition and a concept image. (Elstak, 2009, p. 2)

## Surveying the Prompts and Selected Responses in the Probe

The Probe consists of two selected response items. The prompts and selected responses are designed to elicit understandings and common difficulties as described in the following table.

| If a student chooses | It is likely that the student |
|---|---|
| 1. b and 2. c (correct responses) | • understands the properties of exponents and how to convert between rational exponents and radicals to simplify expressions. [See Sample Student Response 1]<br><br>*Look for indication of the student's understanding in the written explanations of how the student got the answer.* |
| 1. a or c | • uses the rational power $\left(\dfrac{3}{2}\right)$ as a multiplier for the base. Students often multiply 4 by 2 then by 3 to get 12 as in choice a, or multiply 4 by 1.5 $\left(\dfrac{3}{2}\right)$ to get 6 as in choice c. [See Sample Student Response 2] |
| 1. d or e | • incorrectly associates a fractional exponent with a fractional answer. [See Sample Student Response 3] |
| 2. a or b | • multiplies all the numbers together as they are next to each other without any computational symbols shown (choice a). In choice b, students overgeneralize from working with exponents of variables and add the exponents before multiplying. [See Sample Student Response 4] |
| 2. d or e | • associates an answer with a fractional exponent but incorrectly translates to a fractional answer. [See Sample Student Response 5] |
| 1. f or 2. f | • does not have an understanding of rational exponents and/or radicals and sees the expressions as unsolvable. In Question 1, students often see a fractional power and think that it is mistakenly written or cannot be solved without a calculator. In Question 2, students often don't realize that $\sqrt[4]{(25)^2}$ can be written as $\sqrt[4]{(25)^2}$ to make simplification easier. [See Sample Student Response 6] |

## *T*eaching Implications and Considerations

Ideas for eliciting more information from students about their understanding and difficulties:

- What do the different numbers in a rational (fractional) exponent mean?
- Can you rewrite $4^{\frac{3}{2}}$ as a radical? Where does each of the numbers go in radical form? Could it be written a different way in radical form? $(\sqrt[2]{4})^3$ or $(\sqrt[2]{4})^3$ Which way is better to use to simplify the expression? Why?

Ideas for planning instruction in response to what you learned from the results of administering the Probe:

- Allow students exploration time on when/how to use rational exponents and/or radicals to solve problems. Rational exponents sometimes allow greater flexibility and are often easier to write than the equivalent radical form. Each way permits you to do calculations that you couldn't with the other. They should be able to convert back and forth with ease.
- Students should explore rational exponents without a calculator first so they build conceptual understanding. Once this foundation is solidified, technology is a great tool to include. Students should explore how to accurately put rational exponents into a calculator as parentheses are often needed.

## Sample Student Responses to Rational Exponents

### Responses That Suggest Understanding

*Sample Student Response 1*

Probe Item 1: Student chose b. 8. This can be rewritten to be $\sqrt[2]{4^3}$. Now you can just do the math. $4^3$ is 64 and then $\sqrt{64}$.

Probe Item 2: Student chose c. 5. This one is opposite. Think about it as $25^{\frac{2}{4}}$, which is the same as $25^{\frac{1}{2}}$, which is easy since it just means $\sqrt{25}$.

### Responses That Suggest Difficulty

*Sample Student Response 2*

Probe Item 1: Student chose c. 6. 3/2 is 1.5 so 4 × 1.5 is 4 + 2, which is 6.

*Sample Student Response 3*

Probe Item 1: Student chose d. $\frac{1}{8}$. The fraction means to put $\frac{1}{\sqrt[2]{4^3}}$. This comes out to $\frac{1}{8}$.

*Sample Student Response 4*

Probe Item 2: Student chose b. 150. It seems too big but I remembered something about adding 4 and 2 when there are powers in and out of the ( ). $25^6$ is 150.

*Sample Student Response 5*

Probe Item 1: Student chose c. 6. I know this is the same as saying $25^{\frac{2}{4}}$. Fractions in exponents mean 1 over the answer so this final answer is 1 over 8.

*Sample Student Response 6*

Probe Item 2: Student chose f. Can't be simplified. It can be a decimal because no regular number times itself 4 times is 25. 2 × 2 × 2 × 2 is 16 and 3 × 3 × 3 × 3 is 81. If the answer is a decimal, then it is already simplified as it is.

## Variation: Rational Exponents

2.2Va

Simplify without using a calculator.

| Circle the correct answer. | Justify your choice. |
|---|---|
| **1.**<br><br>**Simplify** $4^{-\frac{3}{2}}$<br><br>a. $-24$   e. $\frac{1}{8}$<br><br>b. $-6$   f. $\frac{1}{6}$<br><br>c. $-\frac{1}{8}$   g. $6$<br><br>d. $-\frac{1}{6}$   h. Can't be simplified | |
| **2.**<br><br>**Simplify** $\left(\sqrt[4]{25}\right)^{-2}$<br><br>a. $-200$   d. $-\frac{1}{5}$<br><br>b. $-50$   e. $\frac{1}{5}$<br><br>c. $-5$   f. Can't be simplified | |

**Variation: Understanding Radicals**

Choose if each statement is true or false and justify your choice.

| Circle the correct answer. | Justify your choice. |
|---|---|
| **1.** $\sqrt{ab}$ can **sometimes** be written as $\sqrt{a} \cdot \sqrt{b}$. <br><br> a. True <br><br> b. False | |
| **2.** $(\sqrt[a]{b})^a$ is **always** equivalent to $b$. <br><br> a. True <br><br> b. False | |
| **3.** $\sqrt[b]{a^b}$ is **always** equivalent to $a$. <br><br> a. True <br><br> b. False | |

*(Continued)*

(Continued)

Choose if each statement is true or false and justify your choice.

| Circle the correct answer. | Justify your choice. |
|---|---|
| **4.**<br><br>$\sqrt{a+b}$ can **never** be written as $\sqrt{a}+\sqrt{b}$.<br><br><br>a. True<br><br>b. False | |
| **5.**<br><br>$\sqrt{a}\cdot\sqrt{b}$ is **sometimes** equal to $a$.<br><br><br>a. True<br><br>b. False | |
| **6.**<br><br>$\sqrt{a}+\sqrt{a}$ is **always** equal to $2\sqrt{a}$<br><br><br>a. True<br><br>b. False | |

## Operating With Matrices

2.3

**1. Which of the following is the simplification of the given matrix expression?**

$$\begin{bmatrix} 3 & 1 & 2 \\ 4 & 2 & 0 \end{bmatrix} \cdot \begin{bmatrix} 5 & 3 \\ 1 & 2 \\ 7 & 6 \end{bmatrix}$$

a. $\begin{bmatrix} 15 & 1 & 14 \\ 12 & 4 & 0 \end{bmatrix}$

b. $\begin{bmatrix} 15 & 12 \\ 1 & 4 \\ 14 & 0 \end{bmatrix}$

c. $\begin{bmatrix} 30 & 23 \\ 22 & 14 \end{bmatrix}$

d. Can't be done

Explain your choice:

**2. Which of the following is the simplification of the given matrix expression?**

$$\begin{bmatrix} 0 & 5 & -2 \\ 1 & -3 & 4 \end{bmatrix} \cdot \begin{bmatrix} 2 & 3 & 6 \\ 6 & -1 & -4 \end{bmatrix}$$

a. $\begin{bmatrix} 0 & 15 & -12 \\ 6 & 3 & -16 \end{bmatrix}$

b. $\begin{bmatrix} 3 \\ -7 \end{bmatrix}$

c. $\begin{bmatrix} 2 & 15 & -12 \\ 6 & 3 & -16 \end{bmatrix}$

d. Can't be done

Explain your choice:

## Teacher Notes: Operating With Matrices

# Questions to Consider About the Key Mathematical Concepts

Can students correctly multiply matrices and recognize when matrix multiplication cannot be performed because of the sizes of the matrices? To what extent do they

- make sense of matrix dimensions, entries, and operations with matrices?
- reason whether two matrices can be multiplied?
- describe the process of multiplying two matrices and why specific dimensions are needed?

---

### Common Core Connection (CCSS.Math.Content.HSN-VM.C.8)

**Grade:** High School

**Domain:** Number and Quantity

**Cluster:**

**Perform operations on matrices and use matrices in applications.**

C8. Add, subtract, and multiply matrices of appropriate dimensions.

---

# Uncovering Student Understanding About the Key Concepts

Using the Operating With Matrices Probe can provide the following information about how the students are thinking about operations on matrices.

*Do they*

- recognize the correct dimensions needed for matrix multiplication (the number of columns in the first matrix needs to be the same as the number of rows in the second matrix)?

- correctly multiply the rows in the first matrix with the columns in the second matrix?

OR

*Do they*

- think matrices of any dimension can be multiplied?

OR

- not understand matrix multiplication to be a specific process?

| *Do they* | | *Do they* |
|---|---|---|
| • understand the result of multiplying a 2 × 3 matrix with a 3 × 2 matrix to be a 2 × 2 matrix? | OR | • think the resulting matrix will be the dimensions of one of the original matrices? |

# Exploring Excerpts From Educational Resources and Related Research

Areas of consideration:

Multiplying two matrices can be challenging for many students. They must be able to indentify which matrices can be multiplied and they often have trouble with the concept that multiplication with matrices is not commutative. (Muschla, Muschla, & Muschla-Berry, 2011, p. 132)

Too often, students view matrices as nothing more than abstract rows and columns with which they demonstrate their arithmetic skills. They need to go beyond these manipulations and acquire the knowledge needed to connect matrices with the real world. (Worrall & Quinn, 2001, p. 46)

Geometric introduction to matrices [can] strengthen students' conceptual understanding of matrix algebra. Such concepts as matrix multiplication seemed easier for students when they were first approached in a visual manner. (Edwards, 2003, p. 48)

# Surveying the Prompts and Selected Responses in the Probe

The Probe consists of two selected response items. The prompts and selected responses are designed to elicit understandings and common difficulties as described below:

| *If a student chooses* | *It is likely that the student* |
|---|---|
| 1. c and 2. d (correct responses) | • understands how to multiply matrices of correct dimensions. The column dimension of the first matrix needs to match the row dimension of the second matrix (the number of columns in the first equals the number of rows in the second). The resulting matrix will be the row dimension of the first and the column dimension of the second. In Example 1, the first matrix is a 2 × 3 and the |

*(Continued)*

(Continued)

| If a student chooses | It is likely that the student |
|---|---|
|  | second is a 3 × 2. As these are dimensions that can be multiplied, the resulting matrix will be a 2 × 2. Each entry in the new matrix is obtained by multiplying the row entries in the first matrix with the column entries in the second matrix, then adding the numbers. For instance, to get the first entry in the resulting matrix, you would do the following computations: (3)(5) + (1)(1) + (2)(7), which equals 15 + 1 + 14 = 30. [See Sample Student Response 1]<br><br>*Look for indication of the student's understanding in the written explanations of how the student got the answer.* |
| 1. a or b | • does not fully understand the concept and process of matrix multiplication. The student is multiplying numbers but not in the correct way. As the process is a bit complicated, students may or may not be on their way to complete understanding. Asking the student clarification questions will help to understand where they are in their understanding. [See Sample Student Response 2] |
| 1. d<br>2. a, b, or c | • does not understand that in order for matrices to be multiplied, the number of column entries in the first matrix needs to be the same as the number of row entries in the second matrix. [See Sample Student Response 3] |

## Teaching Implications and Considerations

Ideas for eliciting more information from students about their understanding and difficulties:

- What are the dimensions of each matrix? Is the number of rows or columns represented first in a matrix dimension? What might help you remember that the first number in a matrix dimension represents the number of rows in the matrix?
- What needs to match in order to multiply matrices? Why?
- If two matrices have appropriate dimensions to be multiplied, how can you tell what the dimensions of the resulting matrix will be? (The number of rows of the first and the number of columns of the second)
- Should you circle the rows or the columns in the first matrix? (rows) Why?
- Should you circle the rows or columns in the second matrix? (columns) Why?
- If you have matrix *A* and matrix *B*, is multiplying *A* times *B* the same as multiplying *B* times *A*? Why or why not?
- If multiplying matrix *A* times matrix *B* is possible, does that automatically mean that multiplying matrix *B* times matrix *A* is also possible?

Ideas for planning instruction in response to what you learned from the results of administering the Probe:

- When talking about entries, use words and notation that will help students know what is being discussed. For example in the second matrix in Question 1, when talking about the entry where the 7 is, say "row 3, column 1." This allows them to become familiar with rows, columns, and the placement of each entry. This also helps when finding the entries in the multiplied matrix. As the final matrix is a 2 × 2, if you are looking for the entry in row 1, column 2, you will be multiplying numbers in row 1 of first matrix with numbers in column 2 of second matrix.
- As the row entries of the first matrix need to be multiplied by the column entries of the second matrix, have students circle the rows in the first matrix and the columns in the second matrix. Colored pencils work well for students who like colors!
- Include letters (variables) when working with computations on matrices. This allows students to think abstractly and allows for discussions on conceptual understanding of the processes being used.
- To build conceptual understanding of operation with matrices, use matrices to explore real-world contexts. The use of technology "allow the students to extend their investigations into more interesting and complex situations without having to continuously complete tedious calculations" (Worrall & Quinn, 2001, p. 49).

## Sample Student Responses to Operating With Matrices

### Responses That Suggest Understanding

*Sample Student Response 1*

Probe Item 1: Student chose c. $\begin{bmatrix} 30 & 23 \\ 22 & 14 \end{bmatrix}$. Match up the numbers. The 30 comes from multiplying 3 × 5 and 1 × 1 and 7 × 2 and then adding those 3 numbers. Just move over to get the next number. Multiply the 3, 1, and the 2 by the 3, 2, and 6 in the next matrix. Finally move to the 4, 2, and 0 and repeat in the same way.

### Responses That Suggest Difficulty

*Sample Student Response 2*

Probe Item 1: Student chose a. $\begin{bmatrix} 0 & 15 & -12 \\ 6 & 3 & -16 \end{bmatrix}$. It's easy. Just multiply each number in the same spot to get a new number.

*Sample Student Response 3*

Probe Item 1: Student chose d. Can't be done. The numbers of rows and columns don't match.

**Variation: Matrices**

Choose if each statement is true or false and justify your choice.

| Circle the correct answer. | Justify your choice. |
|---|---|
| **1.**<br><br>**Matrix multiplication is commutative.**<br><br><br>a. True<br><br>b. False | |
| **2.**<br><br>**Every matrix has an inverse matrix.**<br><br><br>a. True<br><br>b. False | |
| **3.**<br><br>**The associate property does not hold for matrix addition.**<br><br><br>a. True<br><br>b. False | |

Choose if each statement is true or false and justify your choice.

| Circle the correct answer. | Justify your choice. |
| --- | --- |
| **4.**<br><br>**Only matrices with the same number of rows and columns can be added or subtracted.**<br><br><br>a. True<br><br>b. False | |
| **5.**<br><br>**All matrices have a determinant.**<br><br><br>a. True<br><br>b. False | |
| **6.**<br><br>**Any two matrices can be multiplied.**<br><br><br>a. True<br><br>b. False | |

# 3

# Algebra Probes

The content of the Probes in this chapter aligns with the standards for high school but is often taught in different courses across districts. The Probes and their variations are also relevant beyond the aligned course level for students in more advanced courses who have not yet met particular standards from previous courses as well as for students who have already met the standards in the current course.

We developed these Probes to address critical areas of focus for high school students, described in the standards (Council of Chief State School Officers [CCSSO], 2010) as follows:

- Use the structure of an expression to identify ways to rewrite it. For example, see $x^4 - y^4$ as $(x^2)^2 - (y^2)^2$, thus recognizing it as a difference of squares that can be factored as $(x^2 - y^2)(x^2 + y^2)$.

- Rewrite simple rational expressions in different forms; write $\frac{a(x)}{b(x)}$ in the form $q(x) + \frac{r(x)}{b(x)}$, where $a(x)$, $b(x)$, $q(x)$, and $r(x)$ are polynomials with the degree of $r(x)$ less than the degree of $b(x)$, using inspection, long division, or, for the more complicated examples, a computer algebra system.

- Solve quadratic equations in one variable.

- Explain each step in solving a simple equation as following from the equality of numbers asserted at the previous step, starting from the assumption that the original equation has a solution. Construct a viable argument to justify a solution method.

The content of the Probes in this chapter aligns with the standards for high school but is often taught in different courses across districts. The Probes and their variations are also relevant beyond the aligned course level for students in more advanced courses who have not yet met particular standards from previous courses as well as for students who have already met the standards in the current course.

- Solve systems of linear equations exactly and approximately (e.g., with graphs), focusing on pairs of linear equations in two variables.
- Represent a system of linear equations as a single matrix equation in a vector variable.

The standards and their related questions, as well as the Probes associated with them, are shown in Table 3.1.

**Table 3.1**  Algebra Probes

| Common Core Mathematical Content | Related Question | Probe Name |
|---|---|---|
| Use the structure of an expression to identify ways to rewrite it. <br><br> CCSS.Math.Content.HSA-SSE.A.2 <br><br> Solve quadratic equations by inspection (e.g., for $x^2 = 49$), taking square roots, completing the square, the quadratic formula, and factoring, as appropriate to the initial form of the equation. <br><br> CCSS.Math.Content.HSA-REI.B.4b | Can students correctly identify equivalent expressions involving exponents? | Equivalent Expressions (p. 53) <br><br> Variation: Is It Simplified? (p. 58) <br><br> Variation: Equivalent Expressions—Trig (p. 59) <br><br> Variation: Equivalent Expressions—Logs (p. 60) |
| Rewrite simple rational expressions in different forms. <br><br> CCSS.Math.Content.HSA-APR.D.6 | Can students use algebraic techniques, including factoring, to correctly simplify rational expressions? | Simplifying Rational Expressions (p. 61) |
| Explain each step in solving a simple equation as following from the equality of numbers asserted at the previous step, starting from the assumption that the original equation has a solution. Construct a viable argument to justify a solution method. <br><br> CCSS.Math.Content.HSA-REI.A.1 | Can students correctly reason about solving equations when the variable is in the denominator? | Solving for a Variable (p. 66) <br><br> Variation: Solving for a Variable (p. 71) <br><br> Variation: Solving for a Variable—Trig (p. 72) |
| Solve quadratic equations by inspection (e.g., for $x^2 = 49$), taking square roots, completing the square, the quadratic formula, and factoring, as appropriate to the initial form of the equation. Recognize when the | When analyzing quadratic equations, can students determine when an equation has real solutions (roots, zeros, $x$-intercepts)? | Solving Quadratic Equations (p. 73) |

*(Continued)*

(Continued)

| Common Core Mathematical Content | Related Question | Probe Name |
|---|---|---|
| quadratic formula gives complex solutions and write them as $a \pm bi$ for real numbers $a$ and $b$.<br><br>*CCSS.Math.Content.HSA-REI.B.4b* | | |
| Solve systems of linear equations exactly and approximately (e.g., with graphs), focusing on pairs of linear equations in two variables.<br><br>*CCSS.Math.Content.HSA-REI.C.6* | Can students analyze pairs of systems of linear equations to determine similarities and differences among their solution sets? | Systems of Linear Equations (p. 78) |
| Represent a system of linear equations as a single matrix equation in a vector variable.<br><br>*CCSS.Math.Content.HSA-REI.C.8* | Can students represent a system of linear equations as a matrix equation? | Matrix Equations (p. 83) |

Take a look at the variations that are available with some of the Probes in this chapter. All of these variations address algebra ideas but may extend the idea or offer a different structure for administering them. When available, variation Probes follow the Teacher Notes and associated reproducibles for the related original Probe.

3.1

## Equivalent Expressions

Decide whether each of the following is an equivalent expression to

$$x^4 - y^4$$

Explain your reasoning on each choice.

---

**A. $(x^2)^2 - (y^2)^2$**    Circle one:    Yes    No    Can't determine

Explain your choice:

---

**B. $(x^2 - y^2)(x^2 + y^2)$**    Circle one:    Yes    No    Can't determine

Explain your choice:

---

**C. $(x + y)(x - y)(x^2 + y^2)$**    Circle one:    Yes    No    Can't determine

Explain your choice:

---

**D. $(x^2 - y^2)^2$**    Circle one:    Yes    No    Can't determine

Explain your choice:

## Teacher Notes:
## Equivalent Expressions

# Questions to Consider About the Key Mathematical Concepts

Can students correctly identify equivalent expressions involving exponents? To what extent do they

- make sense of how expressions involving exponents can be rewritten to create equivalent expressions?
- reason whether certain expressions are equivalent to a given expression?
- describe the process of rewriting an expression to create equivalent ones using the properties of exponents and difference of squares?

## Common Core Connection
## (CCSS.Math.Content.HSA-SSE.A.2)

**Grade:** High School

**Domain:** Algebra

**Cluster:**

**Interpret the structure of expressions.**

A2. Use the structure of an expression to identify ways to rewrite it. For example, see $x^4 - y^4$ as $(x^2)^2 - (y^2)^2$, thus recognizing it as a difference of squares that can be factored as $(x^2 - y^2)(x^2 + y^2)$.

## Common Core Connection
## (CCSS.Math.Content.HSA-REI.B.4b)

**Grade:** High School

**Domain:** Algebra

**Cluster:**

**Solve equations and inequalities in one variable.**

B4b. Solve quadratic equations by inspection (e.g., for $x^2 = 49$), taking square roots, completing the square, the quadratic formula, and factoring, as appropriate to the initial form of the equation.

## $U$ncovering Student Understanding About the Key Concepts

Using the Equivalent Expressions Probe can provide the following information about how the students are thinking about equivalent expressions involving exponents.

| *Do they* | | *Do they* |
|---|---|---|
| • apply the properties of exponents correctly? | OR | • inappropriately apply the properties of exponents? |
| • recognize when the difference of squares can be used to factor or rewrite an expression? | OR | • not realize that an expression can be factored or rewritten? |
| • recognize when expressions are or are not equivalent and why? | OR | • base their opinions on what "looks" equivalent? |

## $E$xploring Excerpts From Educational Resources and Related Research

Areas of consideration:

The expression $(x + y)^2$ is often converted to $x^2 + y^2$ following the pattern of $(xy)^2 = x^2y^2$. Of course writing $(x + y)^2 = (x + y)(x + y)$ and using the distributive law (twice) helps clarify where the missing middle term $2xy$ comes from, in contrast to $(xy)^2$, which converts to $x^2y^2$ using only the commutative and associative laws. (National Council of Teachers of Mathematics [NCTM], 1999, p. 336)

As stated in the Algebra Standard for grades 9 through 12, high school students are expected to "understand the meaning of equivalent forms of expressions, equations, inequalities, and relations" (p. 296). If that understanding is to occur, teachers must figure out how to open classroom discussions to questions about equivalence— to questions about why some methods preserve equivalence and others do not. (NCTM, 2003, p. 123)

Many students have difficulty reading an expression. [They] cannot attach meaning to algebraic expressions. (Stepans, Schmidt, Welsh, Reins, & Saigo, 2005, p. 150)

In general, if students engage extensively in symbolic manipulation before they develop a solid conceptual foundation for their work, they will be unable to do more than mechanical manipulation. The foundation for meaningful work with symbolic notation should be laid over a long time. (NCTM, 2000, p. 39)

## Surveying the Prompts and Selected Responses in the Probe

The Probe consists of four related justified list items. The prompts and selected responses are designed to elicit understandings and common difficulties as described below:

| If a student chooses | It is likely that the student |
|---|---|
| A. Yes, B. Yes, C. Yes, and D. No (correct responses) | • understands how to use the properties of exponents and the difference of squares to write equivalent expressions.<br><br>   ○ In example A, the terms $x^4$ and $y^4$ are rewritten as a power to a power $(x^2)^2$ and $(y^2)^2$.<br>   ○ In example B, the original expression is factored using the difference of squares.<br>   ○ Example C is factored one more time from example B. The difference of squares is used twice to completely factor the original expression. [See Sample Student Response 1]<br><br>*Look for indication of the student's understanding in the written explanations of how the student got the answer.* |
| A. No or Can't determine<br><br>B. No or Can't determine<br><br>C. No or Can't determine | • lacks complete understanding of the properties of exponents and/or does not recognize factored forms of expressions. [See Sample Student Response 2] |
| D. Yes or Can't determine | • inappropriately applies a power into parentheses containing more than one term. Students are probably overgeneralizing the rule that allows $(x^2y^2)^2 = x^4y^4$. [See Sample Student Response 3] |

## Teaching Implications and Considerations

Ideas for eliciting more information from students about their understanding and difficulties:

- What does $x^2$ mean ($x$ times $x$)? What does $(x^2)^2$ mean ($x^2$ times $x^2$)? How many $x$s are being multiplied in this expression ($x$ times $x$ times $x$ times $x$)? How can four $x$s multiplied together be written?
- Expand $(xy)^2$ and $(x + y)^2$. What does each expression mean?
- Compare and contrast $(xy)^2$ and $(x + y)^2$.

- How is the difference of squares used with numbers? What happens when we use variables instead of numbers? In what way is the process the same/different?
- Can the difference of squares be used more than once in an expression?
- What does it mean to have an expression factored completely?

Ideas for planning instruction in response to what you learned from the results of administering the Probe:

- Provide opportunities for students to explore the properties of exponents with numbers before transferring the properties to variables. Investigate equivalent expressions with number bases before working with variable bases.
- With the use of technology, have students compare and contrast the graph of the original expression with the graphs of the other expressions. This can be a starting point for discussions on what makes each one equivalent or not.
- Have students expand (multiply) the expressions in examples B, C, and D to check for equivalency.

## Sample Student Responses to Equivalent Expressions

### Responses That Suggest Understanding

*Sample Student Response 1*

Probe Item A: Student chose Yes. Since $x^4$ is the same as $(x^2)^4$ and same for the $y$ part, then this is equivalent. I checked with whole numbers to be sure.

### Responses That Suggest Difficulty

*Sample Student Response 2*

Probe Item C: Student chose No. This has way too many terms to multiply to be just $x^4 - y^4$.

*Sample Student Response 3*

Probe Item D: Student chose Yes. Just distribute the 2 to each of the inside exponents.

## Variation: Is It Simplified?

3.1Va

Circle the examples showing an appropriate use of "canceling digits" to simply an expression.

**A.**

$$\frac{\cancel{x}y}{\cancel{x}z} = \frac{y}{z}$$

**B.**

$$\frac{\cancel{m}+x}{\cancel{m}+n} = \frac{x}{n}$$

**C.**

$$\frac{\cancel{5}y}{\cancel{5}z} = \frac{y}{z}$$

**D.**

$$\frac{\cancel{c}d}{a\cancel{c}} = \frac{d}{a}$$

**E.**

$$\frac{3\cancel{m}+6n}{5\cancel{m}} = \frac{3+6n}{5}$$

**F.**

$$\frac{5\cancel{xy}z}{7\cancel{xy}} = \frac{z}{7}$$

Explain how you decide which one(s) to circle.

**Variation: Equivalent Expressions—Trig**

Decide whether each of the following are equivalent expressions. Explain your reasoning on each choice.

---

**A. Is sin 3x equivalent to 3 sin x?**

Circle one:　　Yes　　No　　Can't determine

Explain your choice:

---

**B. Is sin x equivalent to $\dfrac{1}{\csc x}$ ?**

Circle one:　　Yes　　No　　Can't determine

Explain your choice:

---

**C. Is sin(x + y) equivalent to sin x + sin y?**

Circle one:　　Yes　　No　　Can't determine

Explain your choice:

---

**D. Is sin π equivalent to sin 3π?**

Circle one:　　Yes　　No　　Can't determine

Explain your choice:

## Variation: Equivalent Expressions—Logs

Decide whether each of the following are equivalent expressions. Explain your reasoning on each choice.

---

**A.** Is $\log x^3$ equivalent to $3 \log x$?

Circle one:     Yes     No     Can't determine

Explain your choice:

---

**B.** Is $\log(x + y)$ equivalent to $\log x + \log y$?

Circle one:     Yes     No     Can't determine

Explain your choice:

---

**C.** Is $\log xy$ equivalent to $x \log y$?

Circle one:     Yes     No     Can't determine

Explain your choice:

---

**D.** Is $\log xy$ equivalent to $\log x + \log y$?

Circle one:     Yes     No     Can't determine

Explain your choice:

## Simplifying Rational Expressions

| Circle the correct answer. | Justify your choice. |
|---|---|
| **1.** Simplify $\dfrac{2x^2-1}{2}$<br><br>a. $x^2 - 1$<br><br>b. $x - 1$<br><br>c. $x^2 - \dfrac{1}{2}$<br><br>d. $x - \dfrac{1}{2}$ | |
| **2.** Simplify $\dfrac{x^2+3x}{x+3}$<br><br>a. $\dfrac{x+3}{3}$<br><br>b. $x$<br><br>c. $2x$<br><br>d. Can't be simplified | |

## Teacher Notes:
## Simplifying Rational Expressions

### Questions to Consider About the Key Mathematical Concepts

Can students use algebraic techniques, including factoring, to correctly simplify rational expressions? To what extent do they

- make sense of when and how rational expressions can be rewritten to allow simplification?
- reason when it is not appropriate to divide out and when it is appropriate to either split a rational expression into more than one term or to factor it to allow for simplification?
- describe the factoring process, if used, and why parts of rational expression can or cannot be divided out?

### Common Core Connection
### (CCSS.Math.Content.HSA-APR.D.6)

**Grade:** High School

**Domain:** Algebra

**Cluster:**

**Rewrite rational expressions.**

D6. Rewrite simple rational expressions in different forms; write $a(x)/b(x)$ in the form $q(x) + r(x)/b(x)$, where $a(x)$, $b(x)$, $q(x)$, and $r(x)$ are polynomials with the degree of $r(x)$ less than the degree of $b(x)$, using inspection, long division, or, for the more complicated examples, a computer algebra system.

### Uncovering Student Understanding About the Key Concepts

Using the Simplifying Rational Expressions Probe can provide the following information about how the students are thinking about simplifying rational expressions.

*Do they*
- realize that common factors are the only parts that can be divided out?
- see the divisor (denominator) as part of all terms in the dividend (numerator)?

OR

*Do they*
- incorrectly divide out common terms?
- not divide all terms in the dividend by all terms in the divisor (use partial division)?

# $E$xploring Excerpts From Educational Resources and Related Research

Areas of consideration:

For most of mathematics through calculus, it happens that misconceptions about fractions provide the root source of many student difficulties. Many of these problems come from fractions not being properly understood (example: Incorrect cancelling of $\frac{ab+c}{b}$ to obtain $a + c$. (Allen, 2007, p. 3)

Even algebra students who are adept at simplifying a variety of polynomial expressions often face a significant challenge when confronted with *rational expressions*—the quotient of two polynomials. There are many possible reasons for this. Perhaps students do not have a solid comprehension of rational numbers and so are unable to handle something that looks like a "fraction with $x$'s in it." Perhaps they are unsure of the order of operations since there may be operations both "above" and "below" the operation of division. Perhaps they have inadequate conceptual understanding of inverse operations and so inappropriately cancel terms. Or perhaps it is something else entirely. Nevertheless, this is important because errors in this domain, according to our experience, are frequent, and algebra students will likely see rational expressions again later in their algebraic career (and certainly if they go on to calculus). (Otten, Males, & Figueras, 2008, p. 1)

# $S$urveying the Prompts and Selected Responses in the Probe

The Probe consists of two selected response items. The prompts and selected responses are designed to elicit understandings and common difficulties as described below:

| If a student chooses | It is likely that the student |
|---|---|
| 1. c and 2. b<br><br>(correct responses) | • understands how to simplify rational expressions to their lowest terms. A rational expression has been reduced to lowest terms if all common factors from the numerator and denominator have been divided out. In Question 1, the terms in the numerator have been split and individually divided by the denominator, so the 2 can be divided out in one of the terms. In Question 2, the numerator ($x^2 + 3x$) can be factored to $x(x + 3)$, and then the $(x + 3)$ can be divided out from the numerator and denominator, leaving an $x$ in the numerator and a 1 in the denominator. [See Sample Student Response 1]<br><br>*Look for indication of the student's understanding in the written explanations of how the student got the answer.* |

*(Continued)*

(Continued)

| If a student chooses | It is likely that the student |
|---|---|
| All other responses | • is using inappropriate dividing out techniques or partial division. [See Sample Student Responses 2 and 3] |

## Teaching Implications and Considerations

Ideas for eliciting more information from students about their understanding and difficulties:

- What is a rational expression? (A fraction in which the numerator and/or denominator are polynomials)
- What are "terms" in a polynomial? How can you tell how many terms there are?
- What is a factor of a number? Of a polynomial?
- How do you factor a number? How do you factor a polynomial?
- How do you know if a polynomial is completely factored?
- How can factoring polynomials help to simplify a rational expression?
- What parts of the dividend need to be divided by the divisor?

Ideas for planning instruction in response to what you learned from the results of administering the Probe:

- As simplifying rational expressions often requires factoring, make sure students have a good understanding of what factors are and how to find them.
- Have students group factored parts with parentheses. Use parentheses even if a polynomial cannot be factored to show students it is one unit and has to be divided out as one unit. This helps them see what parts from the numerator and denominator can or cannot be divided out. Dividing out can only happen if you find a "1" written in disguise.
- Once students learn how to factor trinomials, they often have difficulty factoring out a greatest common factor (GCF) in a polynomial. Throughout the trinomial unit, consistently review the GCF and use it often as a starting place for factoring.
- Difficulties often arise with similar-looking factors like $(x - 2)$ and $(2 - x)$. Give students extended opportunities to explore these types of polynomials. Have them substitute numbers in to see if they produce the same results.
- Once students have decided on a simplified expression, have them substitute the same number in the original expression and their simplified one to see if the results are the same.

- Students should have exposure to rational expressions that cannot be simplified. This allows them to truly understand the process and have discussions on why the expression is already in simplified form.
- This is a great unit or series of lessons to talk about domain and range. It allows students to reflect on what they already know about numbers and transfer their knowledge to polynomials.

## Sample Student Responses to Simplifying Rational Expressions

### Responses That Suggest Understanding

*Sample Student Response 1*

Probe Item 1: Student chose c. $x^2 - \dfrac{1}{2}$. I divided both terms by 2. And got $x^2 - .5$ and then changed .5 back to a fraction.

Probe Item 2: Student chose c. $x$. First I factored an $x$ from the terms and got $x(x + 3)$. $x + 3$ in both places is like dividing something by itself, which is always 1. This leaves the $x$.

### Responses That Suggest Difficulty

*Sample Student Response 2*

Probe Item 1: Student chose a. $x^2 - 1$. I canceled the 2s and everything else stays.

*Sample Student Response 3*

Probe Item 2: Student chose c. $2x$. I canceled $\dfrac{x^2 + 3x}{x + 3}$, then added the two $x$s.

## Solving for a Variable

Students were asked to solve for $x$ in the following equation.

$$36 = \frac{12}{x}$$

Three students have each solved the problem differently.

| Student **A** | Student **B** | Student **C** |
|---|---|---|
| $36 = \dfrac{12}{x}$ | $36 = \dfrac{12}{x}$ | $36 = \dfrac{12}{x}$ |
| $12\,(36) = x$ | $\dfrac{36}{12} = x$ | $\dfrac{12}{36} = x$ |
| $x = 432$ | $x = 3$ | $x = \dfrac{1}{3}$ |

Circle the student you think correctly solved for $x$.

Explain your choice:

## Teacher Notes: Solving for a Variable

### Questions to Consider About the Key Mathematical Concepts

Can students correctly reason about solving equations when the variable is in the denominator? To what extent do they

- make sense of possible solutions to an equation with the variable in the denominator?
- reason about preserving equality and the accuracy of given solutions?
- describe correct solution methods and the errors in incorrect solutions?

### Common Core Connection (CCSS.Math.Content.HSA-REI.A.1)

**Grade:** High School

**Domain:** Algebra

**Cluster:**

**Understand solving equations as a process of reasoning and explain the reasoning.**

A1. Explain each step in solving a simple equation as following from the equality of numbers asserted at the previous step, starting from the assumption that the original equation has a solution. Construct a viable argument to justify a solution method.

### Uncovering Student Understanding About the Key Concepts

Using the Solving for a Variable Probe can provide the following information about how the students are thinking about solving for a variable in the denominator.

| *Do they* | | *Do they* |
|---|---|---|
| • recognize correct and incorrect solutions to an equation? | OR | • not recognize errors in certain solutions? |
| • see relationships between numbers and variables in an equation? | OR | • see the numbers and letters disconnected from each other? |

| *Do they* | | *Do they* |
|---|---|---|
| • preserve equality while manipulating the numbers and/or variable? | OR | • ignore the equality and incorrectly manipulate the numbers and/or variable? |
| • understand that the variable $x$ needs to be moved to the numerator to solve the equation (by multiplying both sides by $x$, cross-multiplying, or flipping both sides of the equation)? | OR | • leave the variable in the denominator and try to "work around it" or just move it up to the numerator without the proper steps? |

# Exploring Excerpts From Educational Resources and Related Research

Areas of consideration:

Algebra students are frequently asked to manipulate symbols according to memorized rules without being asked to consider what these symbols might represent. (Stephens, 2003, p. 65)

Every year I am faced with the same dilemma of how can I structure a lesson on solving rational equations that encourages problem solving and reasoning. The study of rational equations is necessary for future mathematics courses, so removing this topic from my syllabus is not an option. To compound this quandary, textbooks typically present procedures for solving rational equations that emphasize algebraic manipulations but exclude reasoning and sense-making. (Smith, 1997, p. 749)

# Surveying the Prompts and Selected Responses in the Probe

The Probe consists of one selected response. The prompts and selected responses are designed to elicit understandings and common difficulties as described below:

| If a student chooses | It is likely that the student |
|---|---|
| Student C (correct response) | • understands the process for solving for an unknown in the denominator. They can manipulate equations to isolate a particular number or variable while preserving equality. [See Sample Student Response 1]<br><br>*Look for indication of the student's understanding in the written explanations of how the student got the answer.* |

| If a student chooses | It is likely that the student |
|---|---|
| Student A | • is solving for *x* by "flipping" the right side of the equation, putting the 12 in the denominator, and then multiplying both sides by 12 to move it to the other side. For this process to work, both sides of the equation would need to be "flipped" to preserve equality. [See Sample Student Response 2] |
| Student B | • is moving the 12 correctly by dividing both sides of the equation by 12 but then is incorrectly placing the variable in the numerator on the right-hand side of the equation. The student loses sight of preserving equality. [See Sample Student Response 3] |

## Teaching Implications and Considerations

Ideas for eliciting more information from students about their understanding and difficulties:

- What do you have to do to 12 to make it equal to 36 pieces?
- What is happening to 12 in this equation? (It is being divided by *x*.) What would or could you do to undo that operation? (Multiply by *x*.)
- If you had $9 = \dfrac{x}{3}$, how would you move the 3 to the other side? What if you had $9 = \dfrac{3}{x}$? Would the process be the same?
- When you substitute your answer in for *x* in the original equation, does it create a true statement (equation)? If it does, what does that tell you about your answer? If it doesn't?

Ideas for planning instruction in response to what you learned from the results of administering the Probe:

- Students should make sense of equations before they start manipulating them. Have them come up with a real-life situation or be able to discuss the equation and what is happening to the numbers and variables.
- Have students look for relationships between numbers or between numbers and variables.
- Many equations can be looked at as a proportion (36 is to one as 12 is to *x*). This gives students a relationship to focus on and an idea of what might need to be done to solve it.
- Students should check their answers to see if it makes sense in the original equation.
- Critiquing wrong solutions and having discussions around them can lead to a deeper understanding of equations and how to correctly (and incorrectly) manipulate them. This allows students' thought processes to move higher on taxonomy tables.

## Sample Student Responses to Solving for a Variable

### Responses That Suggest Understanding

*Sample Student Response 1*

Probe Item: Student chose Student C. It is $\frac{12}{36}$ because the only way to divide 12 by a number and get 36 is if that number is $\frac{1}{3}$. You can also think about it as 36 times something is 12.

### Responses That Suggest Difficulty

*Sample Student Response 2*

Probe Item: Student chose Student A. Solve it by doing the opposite since it is 12 divided by $x$, then multiply instead.

*Sample Student Response 3*

Probe Item: Student chose Student B. I divided both sides by 12. The 12s on the side with the $x$ cancel.

## Variation: Solving for a Variable

Students were asked to solve for $x$ in the following equation.

$$\frac{10}{x+3} = 4$$

Three students have each solved the problem differently.

| Student **A** | Student **B** | Student **C** |
|---|---|---|
| $\frac{10}{x+3} = 4$ | $\frac{10}{x+3} = 4$ | $\frac{10}{x+3} = 4$ |
| $x + 3 = 40$ | $4x + 12 = 10$ | $x + 12 = 10$ |
| $x = 37$ | $x = -\frac{1}{2}$ | $x = -2$ |

Circle the student you think correctly solved for $x$.

Explain your choice:

**Variation: Solving for a Variable—Trig**

Students were asked to solve for $x$ in the following equation.

$$\sin 32 = \frac{12}{x}$$

Three students have each solved the problem differently.

| | | |
|---|---|---|
| $\sin 32 = \dfrac{12}{x}$ | $\sin 32 = \dfrac{12}{x}$ | $\sin 32 = \dfrac{12}{x}$ |
| $12 \sin 32 = x$ | | $x \sin 32 = 12$ |
| $x = 12 \sin 32$ | $\sin \dfrac{32}{12} = x$ | $x = \dfrac{12}{\sin 32}$ |
| Student **A** | Student **B** | Student **C** |

Circle the student you think correctly solved for $x$.

Explain your choice:

## Solving Quadratic Equations

Without graphing, decide whether each of the following quadratics have real solutions.

| | | |
|---|---|---|
| **A.** $y = 2x^2 - 3x + 4$ | Circle one: | Yes No |
| Explain your choice: | | |

| | | |
|---|---|---|
| **B.** $y = 9x^2 + 12 + 4$ | Circle one: | Yes No |
| Explain your choice: | | |

| | | |
|---|---|---|
| **C.** $y = x(-4x + 5) + 1$ | Circle one: | Yes No |
| Explain your choice: | | |

| | | |
|---|---|---|
| **D.** $y = -2x^2 + 6x - 10$ | Circle one: | Yes No |
| Explain your choice: | | |

| | | |
|---|---|---|
| **E.** $y = (x + 3)^2 - 2$ | Circle one: | Yes No |
| Explain your choice: | | |

## Teacher Notes: Solving Quadratic Equations

## Questions to Consider About the Key Mathematical Concepts

When analyzing quadratic equations, can students determine when an equation has real solutions (roots, zeros, $x$-intercepts)? To what extent do they

- make sense of the relationship between an equation and its solutions?
- apply both graphing and nongraphing methods for determining whether a quadratic equation has real or complex solutions?
- describe how to determine whether a solution is real or complex?

### Common Core Connection (CCSS.Math.Content.HSA-REI.B.4b)

**Grade:** High School

**Domain:** Algebra

**Cluster:**

**Solve equations and inequalities in one variable.**

4B. Solve quadratic equations by inspection (e.g., for $x^2 = 49$), taking square roots, completing the square, the quadratic formula, and factoring, as appropriate to the initial form of the equation. Recognize when the quadratic formula gives complex solutions and write them as $a \pm bi$ for real numbers $a$ and $b$.

## Uncovering Student Understanding About the Key Concepts

Using the Solving Quadratic Equations Probe can provide the following information about how the students are thinking about the meaning of solutions to quadratic equations. Although graphing methods are considered important and appropriate, the Probe elicits whether students understand additional solutions methods and what this means in terms of real or complex solutions.

*Do they*

- make sense of the relationship between the equation and its solutions?

OR

*Do they*

- solve the equation correctly but misinterpret what the solution means in terms of real or complex solutions?

| *Do they* | | *Do they* |
|---|---|---|
| • correctly apply a nongraphing solution technique? | OR | • revert to graphing as a solution method or<br>• incorrectly apply a nongraphing solution technique? |

# Exploring Excerpts From Educational Resources and Related Research

Areas of consideration:

There are three commonly used forms for a quadratic expression: Standard form (e.g. $x^2 - 2x - 3$); Factored form (e.g. $(x + 1)(x - 3)$) and Vertex (or complete square) form (e.g. $(x - 1)^2 - 4$). Each is useful in different ways. The traditional emphasis on simplification as an automatic procedure might lead students to automatically convert the second two forms to the first, before considering which form is most useful in a given context. This can lead to time consuming detours in algebraic work, such as solving by first expanding and then applying the quadratic formula. (Common Core Standards Writing Team, 2013a, p. 4)

It is traditional for students to spend a lot of time on various techniques of solving quadratic equations, which are often presented as if they are completely unrelated (factoring, completing the square, the quadratic formula). . . . Rather than long drills on techniques of dubious value, students with an understanding of the underlying reasoning behind all these methods are opportunistic in their application, choosing the method that bests suits the situation at hand. (Common Core Standards Writing Team, 2013a, p. 11)

For many secondary school students, solving quadratic equations is one of the most conceptually challenging subjects in the curriculum (Vaiyavutjamai, Ellerton, & Clements, 2005). In Turkey, where a national mathematics curriculum for elementary and secondary levels is implemented, the teaching and learning of quadratic equations are introduced through factorization, the quadratic formula, and completing the square by using symbolic algorithms. Of these techniques, students typically prefer factorization when the quadratic is obviously factorable. With this technique, students can solve the quadratic equations quickly without paying attention to their structure and conceptual meaning (Sönnerhed, 2009). However, as Taylor and Mittag (2001) suggest, the factorization technique is only symbolic in its nature. Since students simply memorize the procedures and formulas to solve quadratic equations, they have little understanding of the meaning of quadratic equations, and do not understand what to do and why. (Gozde, Bas, & Erbas, 2012, p. 1)

## Surveying the Prompts and Selected Responses in the Probe

The Probe consists of five selected response items. The prompts and selected responses are designed to elicit understandings and common difficulties as described below:

| If a student chooses | It is likely that the student |
|---|---|
| A. No, B. Yes, C. Yes, D. No, and E. Yes (correct responses) | • is able to determine if the solution is real or complex. Look for student explanations that use nongraphing techniques, including factoring and finding the value of the determinant. [See Sample Student Response 1]<br><br>*Look for indication of the student's understanding in the written explanations of how the student got the answer.* |
| C. No and E. No | • is focusing on the form of the equation and is associating only standard forms with having real solutions. [See Sample Student Response 2] |
| C. No and D. No | • incorrectly associates negative coefficients of the $x^2$ term with nonreal solutions. [See Sample Student Response 3] |
| B. No | • incorrectly associates a zero discriminant with nonreal solutions. [See Sample Student Response 4] |
| Miscellaneous other choices | • chooses No when having difficulty using a factoring approach.<br>• makes an error when finding the discriminant or using the quadratic formula. |

## Teaching Implications and Considerations

Ideas for eliciting more information from students about their understanding and difficulties:

- For students having difficulty with factoring, ask, "What solution methods might help you determine the types of solutions?"
- For students who apply the quadratic formula, ask, "How might you determine whether the solutions are real or complex without finding the actual solutions?"
- For students who are only looking at the form of the equation, ask, "How can this equation be written in a different form?"
- Ask the student to graph the equation and compare the results.

Ideas for planning instruction in response to what you learned from the results of administering the Probe:

- When graphing quadratic equations to determine solutions, return students' attention to the original form of the equation to help them form generalizations.

- Provide opportunities for students to see many examples and non-examples of quadratic equations with real solutions, varying the form of the original equation presented.
- Use the terms *roots, zeros, solutions,* and *x-intercepts* so students know how they are interchangeable.
- Focus on the underlying reasoning behind the different methods of solving quadratic equations.

## Sample Student Responses to Solving Quadratic Equations

### Responses That Suggest Understanding

*Sample Student Response 1*

Selects all correct answers

Probe Item A: Student chose No. I used the $b^2 - 4ac$ part of the quadratic formula. Since this equals −13, the solutions are not real since $\sqrt{-13}$ is an imaginary number.

### Responses That Suggest Difficulty

*Sample Student Response 2*

Probe Item C: Student chose No. This isn't a quadratic equation.

*Sample Student Response 3*

Probe Item D: Student chose No. The $x^2$ number is negative, so it won't cross the axis.

*Sample Student Response 4*

Probe Item B: Student chose No. Solved for $\sqrt{b^2 - 4ac}$ and got zero.

**Systems of Linear Equations**

Look at the sets of systems of linear equations.

| Circle the set with a solution that differs from the others. | Justify your choice. |
|---|---|
| 1.<br><br>a. $y = 3x - 4$<br><br>$2y - 6x = -8$<br><br>b. $y = \frac{1}{2}x + 3$<br><br>$4y - 2x = 10$<br><br>c. $y = -2x + 8$<br><br>$3y + 6x = 24$ | |
| 2.<br><br>a. $y = 3x - 4$<br><br>$2y - 6x = 5$<br><br>b. $y = \frac{3}{4}x - 2$<br><br>$3y + 4x = 1$<br><br>c. $y = -\frac{5}{2}x + 3$<br><br>$5y - 2x = 8$ | |
| 3.<br><br>a. $y = 6x - 4$<br><br>$y = 4x + 6$<br><br>b. $y = \frac{1}{2}x + 3$<br><br>$y = \frac{1}{2}x + 4$<br><br>c. $y = 2x + 5$<br><br>$y = -3x + 1$ | |

# Teacher Notes: Systems of Linear Equations

## Questions to Consider About the Key Mathematical Concepts

Can students analyze pairs of systems of linear equations to determine similarities and differences among their solution sets? To what extent do they

- make sense of pairs of linear equations to look for similarities and differences in slope and *y*-intercept?
- distinguish between systems with one solution point, no solution point, and infinitely many solution points?

---

### Common Core Connection (CCSS.Math.Content.HSA-REI.C.6)

**Grade:** High School

**Domain:** Algebra

**Cluster:**

**Solve systems of equations.**

C6. Solve systems of linear equations exactly and approximately (e.g., with graphs), focusing on pairs of linear equations in two variables.

---

## Uncovering Student Understanding About the Key Concepts

Using the Systems of Linear Equations Probe can provide the following information about how the students are thinking about analyzing systems of linear equations and their solutions.

*Do they*

- look at the slopes and *y*-intercepts to determine types of solutions?

OR

- distinguish between the solutions to determine which is different?

*Do they*

- rely on using a method to solve each system before choosing the pair that does not belong?

OR

- focus on unrelated features (such as form of the equations)?

## Exploring Excerpts From Educational Resources and Related Research

Areas of consideration:

For [some] students the concept of *solution* developed out of the action of solving the equation (or system of equations), rather than the action of substitution. By this we mean the solving methods (algorithms) they used (such as Gaussian elimination, or any other). Such algorithms are difficult to interiorize, and do not make it easy for the student to predict the form of the outcome, the solution, without actually calculating it. . . . For these students, *solution* as *solving* is at the Action level of development, and we know that when a concept is still at that level of its development, the student can only perform the action one step at a time. Hence their tendency to start solving when asked about the solutions. Another characteristic of his level is that the student has no ability to predict the outcome without actually performing the action. Here—the students could not predict the mathematical form of the solution, of the outcome of the solving procedure, before they actually carried it out. (Lagasse, 2012, p. 33)

There are very few references addressing the issue of student understanding of systems of linear equation. There is, however, related literature in linear algebra on how to alleviate students' difficulties. In the general literature, one attempt to reduce the difficulties in learning linear algebra is the push for the connection of the topics in linear algebra to real-life applications. For example, "Too often, students view matrices as nothing more than abstract rows and columns with which they demonstrate their arithmetic skills. They need to go beyond these manipulations and acquire the knowledge needed to connect matrices with the real world" (Worrall, & Quinn, 2001, p. 46). In the case of systems of linear equations, understanding the connections that solutions have with original systems, whether it is contextual, algebraic, or graphical, may lead to deeper meaning for the student. (Ramirez, 2009, p. 3)

## Surveying the Prompts and Selected Responses in the Probe

The Probe consists of three separate items, each with three pairs of systems of linear equations. The prompts and selected responses are designed to elicit understandings and common difficulties as described below:

| *If a student chooses* | *It is likely that the student* |
|---|---|
| 1. b, 2. a, and 3. b (correct responses) | • recognizes that in Problem 1, b represents parallel lines where a and c represent coinciding lines. |

| If a student chooses | It is likely that the student |
|---|---|
| | • recognizes that in Problem 2, a represents parallel lines where b and c represent perpendicular lines.<br>• recognizes that in Problem 3, b represents parallel lines where a and c represent lines with exactly one solution point. [See Sample Student Response 1]<br><br>*Look for indication of the student's understanding in the written explanations of how the student got the answer.* |
| Various other patterns | • has done one of the following:<br>  ○ made an error when transforming to an alternate form or when determining slope and *y*-intercept. [See Sample Student Response 2]<br>  ○ focused on unrelated features such as "the only one with a fraction as a slope." [See Sample Student Response 3] |

## *T*eaching Implications and Considerations

Ideas for eliciting more information from students about their understanding and difficulties:

- What features of equations of lines can be looked at for comparison?
- How can you tell what the slope and *y*-intercept of each equation is? What if the equations are not written in slope-intercept form?
- What can you determine about the slope and *y*-intercept of each of these lines?
- What do the graphs of each equation look like?
- How are the equations of parallel lines similar? Different?
- How many solutions are there in a system of equations with parallel lines?
- How are the equations of perpendicular lines similar? Different?
- How many solutions are there in a system of equations with perpendicular lines?
- How are the equations of coinciding lines similar? Different?
- How many solutions are there in a system of equations with coinciding lines?
- Tell me more about how you are comparing the three systems of equations.

Ideas for planning instruction in response to what you learned from the results of administering the Probe:

- Use technology as an avenue for students to make connections between the graphs of systems of equations and their algebraic representations.

- Provide multiple opportunities for students to work within a context for coinciding, perpendicular, parallel, and intersecting lines.
- Use examples and nonexamples for coinciding, perpendicular, parallel, and intersecting lines represented in all forms: contexts, tables, graphs, and equations.
- Have students create and represent sets of linear equations when given conditions (i.e., create two different systems of linear equations in which the lines are perpendicular).

## Sample Student Responses to Systems of Linear Equations

### Responses That Suggest Understanding

*Sample Student Response 1*

Probe Item 1: Student chose b. I looked at the slope and *y*-intercept. b is different because same slope and different *y*-intercepts mean parallel lines. The other two, a and c, are just the same line once you simplify everything.

### Responses That Suggest Difficulty

*Sample Student Response 2*

Probe Item 2: Student chose c. The lines in a and b are parallel since in a, the slopes are both 3, and in b, the slopes are both $\frac{3}{4}$.

*Sample Student Response 3*

Probe Item 2: Student chose a. This is the only one with slopes that are not fractions.

### Matrix Equations

Given the following System of Equations, decide whether each matrix equation accurately represents the system.

$$3x + 2y = 14 \qquad y - 4x = -6$$

**A.** $\begin{bmatrix} 3 & 1 \\ 2 & -4 \end{bmatrix} \cdot \begin{bmatrix} x \\ y \end{bmatrix} = \begin{bmatrix} 14 \\ -6 \end{bmatrix}$    Circle one:    Yes    No

Explain your choice:

---

**B.** $\begin{bmatrix} 3 & 2 \\ 1 & -4 \end{bmatrix} \cdot \begin{bmatrix} x \\ y \end{bmatrix} = \begin{bmatrix} 14 \\ -6 \end{bmatrix}$    Circle one:    Yes    No

Explain your choice:

---

**C.** $\begin{bmatrix} 3 & 2 \\ -4 & 1 \end{bmatrix} \cdot \begin{bmatrix} x \\ y \end{bmatrix} = \begin{bmatrix} 14 \\ -6 \end{bmatrix}$    Circle one:    Yes    No

Explain your choice:

---

**D.** $\begin{bmatrix} 3x & 1y \\ 2x & -4y \end{bmatrix} \cdot \begin{bmatrix} x \\ y \end{bmatrix} = \begin{bmatrix} 14 \\ -6 \end{bmatrix}$    Circle one:    Yes    No

Explain your choice:

---

**E.** $\begin{bmatrix} 2 & 3 \\ 1 & -4 \end{bmatrix} \cdot \begin{bmatrix} y \\ x \end{bmatrix} = \begin{bmatrix} 14 \\ -6 \end{bmatrix}$    Circle one:    Yes    No

Explain your choice:

# Teacher Notes:
# Matrix Equations

## Questions to Consider About the Key Mathematical Concepts

Can students represent a system of linear equations as a matrix equation? To what extent do they

- make sense of the relationship between algebraic and matrix equations?
- reason about the accuracy of matrix equations representing a given system of equations?
- describe their reasoning of the accuracy or inaccuracy of matrix representations using matrix multiplication?

---

### Common Core Connection
### (CCSS.Math.Content.HSA-REI.C.8)

**Grade:** High School

**Domain:** Algebra

**Cluster:**

**Solve systems of equations.**

C8. Represent a system of linear equations as a single matrix equation in a vector variable.

---

## Uncovering Student Understanding About the Key Concepts

Using the Matrix Equations Probe can provide the following information about how the students are thinking about using matrices to solve systems of equations.

| *Do they* | | *Do they* |
|---|---|---|
| • understand where the coefficients of the variables need to be placed in a matrix equation? | OR | • place the numbers in the matrices as they appear in the equation (i.e., always applies a direct translation)? |
| • understand how matrices are multiplied so if the variable matrix is changed, then the coefficient matrix also needs to be changed? | OR | • not see the multiplicative connection between the two matrices (usually on the left side of equation)? |

# *E*xploring Excerpts From Educational Resources and Related Research

Areas of consideration:

Too often, students view matrices as nothing more than abstract rows and columns with which they demonstrate their arithmetic skills. They need to go beyond these manipulations and acquire the knowledge needed to connect matrices with the real world. (Worrall & Quinn, 2001, p. 46)

Researchers have already pointed to concepts such as subspaces, span, bases, linear independence and dependence, linear transformation, and matrices as areas of difficulty for students in linear algebra (Medina, 2000; Hristovitch, 2001). (Ramirez, 2009, p. 3)

According to Action, Process, Object and Schema process, the development of every concept begins in the learner's mind with an action. At this level the learner can only perform the action one step at a time. For example, given a system of linear equations with $n$ unknowns, as well as several [lists of elements] and matrices of different sizes, students are asked which of the givens is a possible solution. If the students start substituting each [element] separately, we suspect that they cannot imagine in advance whether a given [element] can be substituted and hence be a prospective solution. The theory accounts for such inability by the explanation that at the action level, the learners are able to complete the action step after step, but cannot think of it as a whole and predict its outcome; sometimes they can also not describe it verbally. (DeVries & Arnon, 2004, p. 55)

# *S*urveying the Prompts and Selected Responses in the Probe

The Probe consists of five selected responses, each related to a common prompt. The prompts and selected responses are designed to elicit understandings and common difficulties as described below:

| *If a student chooses* | *It is likely that the student* |
|---|---|
| A. No, B. No, C. Yes, D. No, E. Yes<br><br>(correct responses) | • understands the relationship between a system of equations and a matrix equation. [See Sample Student Response 1]<br><br>*Look for indication of the student's understanding in the written explanations of how the student got the answer.* |
| A. Yes, B. Yes, C. No, D. Yes, E. No | • lacks understanding of the placement of the variable coefficients in a matrix equation. [See Sample Student Response 2]<br>• is overgeneralizing from "$x$ must come first." [See Sample Student Response 3] |

## Teaching Implications and Considerations

Ideas for eliciting more information from students about their understanding and difficulties:

- How do you multiply two matrices? Which number in the first matrix would be multiplied by which variable in the second matrix of each example?
- How are linear equations usually written (standard form of $ax + by = c$)? Are both of the equations in the given system written in standard form? If not, can you put them in standard form?
- What are the coefficients of the variables in the algebraic equations?
- Where should the coefficient of $x$ be placed to ensure that it will be multiplied by the $x$ in a matrix equation? What about the coefficient of $y$?

Ideas for planning instruction in response to what you learned from the results of administering the Probe:

- Connect systems of equations/matrix equations to real-life situations.
- When teaching and learning about matrix multiplication, use variables in at least one of the matrices so students see the results of multiplying a number matrix by a variable matrix.
- Circle the rows in the first matrix and the columns in the second matrix each time you multiple matrices until this process is natural to students. Many students will need to do this each time, and that is fine.
- Sometimes students will retain this concept better if they are given a matrix equation to multiple out and discover an algebraic equation or system of equations waiting for them.

### Sample Student Responses to Matrix Equations

**Responses That Suggest Understanding**

*Sample Student Response 1*

Probe Item E: Student chose Yes. If you just rewrite the first equation as $2y + 3x = 14$ (commutative property), then this setup works the same as the one in C.

**Responses That Suggest Difficulty**

*Sample Student Response 2*

Probe Item B: Student chose Yes. The numbers are all in the same order as they are in the equations.

*Sample Student Response 3*

Probe Item E: Student chose No. You are supposed to use standard form, which means the $x$ always comes first.

# 4

# Functions Probes

The content of the Probes in this chapter aligns with the standards for high school but is often taught in different courses across districts. The Probes and their variations are also relevant beyond the aligned course level for students in more advanced courses who have not yet met particular standards from previous courses as well as for students who have already met the standards in the current course.

We developed these Probes to address this critical area of focus for high school students, described in the standards (Council of Chief State School Officers [CCSSO], 2010) as follows:

- For a function that models a relationship between two quantities, interpret key features of graphs and tables in terms of the quantities, and sketch graphs showing key features given a verbal description of the relationship.
- Identify the effect on the graph of replacing $f(x)$ by $f(x) + k$, $k\,f(x)$, $f(kx)$, and $f(x + k)$ for specific values of $k$ (both positive and negative); find the value of $k$ given the graphs. Experiment with cases and illustrate an explanation of the effects on the graph using technology. Include recognizing even and odd functions from their graphs and algebraic expressions for them.
- Explain how the unit circle in the coordinate plane enables the extension of trigonometric functions to all real numbers, interpreted as radian measures of angles traversed counterclockwise around the unit circle.
- Construct linear and exponential functions, including arithmetic and geometric sequences, given a graph, a description of a relationship, or two input-output pairs (include reading these from a table).

The content of the Probes in this chapter aligns with the standards for high school but is often taught in different courses across districts. The Probes and their variations are also relevant beyond the aligned course level for students in more advanced courses who have not yet met particular standards from previous courses as well as for students who have already met the standards in the current course.

- For exponential models, express as a logarithm the solution to $ab^{ct} = d$, where $a$, $c$, and $d$ are numbers and the base $b$ is 2, 10, or e; evaluate the logarithm using technology.
- Understand the inverse relationship between exponents and logarithms and use this relationship to solve problems involving logarithms and exponents.

The standards and their related questions, as well as the Probes associated with them, are shown in Table 4.1.

**Table 4.1**   Functions Probes

| Common Core Mathematical Content | Related Question | Probe Name |
|---|---|---|
| For a function that models a relationship between two quantities, interpret key features of graphs and tables in terms of the quantities, and sketch graphs showing key features given a verbal description of the relationship. <br><br> *CCSS.Math.Content.HSF-IF.B.4* | When interpreting graphs and verbal descriptions, do students understand and use key descriptive features instead of interpreting graphs as literal pictures? | Jogging: Graphical Representation (p. 90) |
| For a function that models a relationship between two quantities, interpret key features of graphs and tables in terms of the quantities, and sketch graphs showing key features given a verbal description of the relationship. Key features include intercepts; intervals where the function is increasing, decreasing, positive, or negative; relative maximums and minimums; symmetries; end behavior; and periodicity. <br><br> *CCSS.Math.Content.HSF-IF.B.4* | When interpreting graphical representations of functions, do students recognize domain intervals where a function is increasing, decreasing, or constant? | Interpreting Functions (p. 96) |
| Identify the effect on the graph of replacing $f(x)$ by $f(x) + k$, $k\,f(x)$, $f(kx)$, and $f(x + k)$ for specific values of $k$ (both positive and negative); find the value of $k$ given the graphs. Experiment with cases and illustrate an explanation of the effects on the graph using technology. Include recognizing even and odd functions from their graphs and algebraic expressions for them. <br><br> *CCSS.Math.Content.HSF-BF.B.3* | When working with functions, do students understand how algebraic representations describe graphical transformations? | Transformation of Functions (p. 101) <br><br> Variation: Transformation of Functions—Trig (p. 106) |

| Common Core Mathematical Content | Related Question | Probe Name |
|---|---|---|
| Understand radian measure of an angle as the length of the arc on the unit circle subtended by the angle.<br><br>*CCSS.Math.Content.HSF-TF.A.1*<br><br>Explain how the unit circle in the coordinate plane enables the extension of trigonometric functions to all real numbers, interpreted as radian measures of angles traversed counterclockwise around the unit circle.<br><br>*CCSS.Math.Content.HSF-TF.A.2* | When solving problems with circular measurements, can students accurately determine an estimate for the measure of an arc drawn in a circle? | Circular Measurement (p. 107) |
| Recognize situations in which one quantity changes at a constant rate per unit interval relative to another.<br><br>*CCSS.Math.Content.HSF-LE.A.1b* | Can students distinguish between examples and nonexamples of direct and inverse relationships? | Direct and Inverse Variation (p. 112)<br><br>Variation: Direct and Inverse Card Sort (p. 118) |
| Construct linear and exponential functions, including arithmetic and geometric sequences, given a graph, a description of a relationship, or two input-output pairs (include reading these from a table).<br><br>*CCSS.Math.Content.HSF-LE.A.2* | When given a graph of an exponential function without labeled intervals, can students determine possible algebraic representations of the graph? | Equation of the Function (p. 120)<br><br>Variation: Equation of the Function (p. 125) |
| For exponential models, express as a logarithm the solution to $ab^{ct} = d$, where $a$, $c$, and $d$ are numbers and the base $b$ is 2, 10, or $e$; evaluate the logarithm using technology.<br><br>*CSS.Math.Content.HSF-LE.A.4*<br><br>Understand the inverse relationship between exponents and logarithms and use this relationship to solve problems involving logarithms and exponents.<br><br>*CCSS.Math.Content.HSF-BF.B.5* | When analyzing logarithms, do students understand how to evaluate a logarithm by first expressing it as an exponential equation? | Logarithms (p. 126) |

Take a look at the variations that are available with some of the Probes in this chapter. All of these variations address ideas about functions but may extend the idea or offer a different structure for administering them. When available, variation Probes follow the Teacher Notes and associated reproducibles for the related original Probe.

## Jogging: Graphical Representation

Adam jogs up a hill at a steady pace. He then runs down the hill at an increased pace. Determine if each graph could describe his running pattern.

| Circle Yes or No. | Explain your choice. |
|---|---|
| **1.** <br><br> Yes      No | |
| **2.** <br><br> Yes      No | |
| **3.** <br><br> Yes      No | |
| **4.** <br><br> Yes      No | |

## Teacher Notes: Jogging: Graphical Representation

## **Q**uestions to Consider About the Key Mathematical Concepts

When interpreting graphs and verbal descriptions, do students understand and use key descriptive features instead of interpreting graphs as literal pictures? To what extent do they

- make sense of the connections between graphical and verbal representations?
- reason about correct and incorrect graphical representations based on a given verbal description?
- describe key features of a verbal description (distance and pace) with those of a graphical representation (direction and rate of change/slope)?

### Common Core Connection (CCSS.Math.Content.HSF-IF.B.4)

**Grade:** High School

**Domain:** Functions

**Cluster:**

**Interpret functions that arise in applications in terms of the context.**

B4. For a function that models a relationship between two quantities, interpret key features of graphs and tables in terms of the quantities, and sketch graphs showing key features given a verbal description of the relationship. *Key features include intercepts; intervals where the function is increasing, decreasing, positive, or negative; relative maximums and minimums; symmetries; end behavior; and periodicity.*

## **U**ncovering Student Understanding About the Key Concepts

Using the Jogging: Graphical Representation Probe can provide the following information about how the students are making connections between verbal and graphical representation.

*Do they*

- understand the relationship between time and distance?

OR

*Do they*

- interpret graphs as literal pictures?

| *Do they* | | *Do they* |
|---|---|---|
| • represent pace from a verbal description as rate of change in the graphical representation? | OR | • see rate of change in the graph as part of the hill in the verbal description? |
| • understand that time without movement is represented graphically as a constant function (horizontal line)? | OR | • see a constant function as walking on a flat surface or walking at a constant pace? |

## Exploring Excerpts From Educational Resources and Related Research

Areas of consideration:

Among the most widely agreed upon conclusions of research on graphing in the last 25 years is that visuality is a key source of difficulties for students using graphs. "Iconic interpretation," that is, interpreting a graph as a literal picture, and other inappropriate responses to visual attributes are "the most frequent cited student errors with respect to interpreting and constructing graphs" (Leinhardt, Zaslavsky, & Stein, 1990, p. 39). (National Council of Teachers of Mathematics [NCTM], 2003, p. 257)

Often students think of the graph as simply a [literal] picture of the scene. (Van Dyke, 2002, p. 5)

Some misconceptions are not so much geometric in nature as they are idiosyncratic to graphing, as when students confuse the picture of the graph with the actual event. For example, it is difficult for students to imagine that a vehicle whose speed is graphed [with a negative slope to represent decrease in speed over time] could be [actually] going uphill. (NCTM, 1999, p. 335)

## Surveying the Prompts and Selected Responses in the Probe

The Probe consists of four selected response items, each relating to a common verbal description. The prompts and selected responses are designed to elicit understandings and common difficulties as described in the following table.

| If a student chooses | It is likely that the student |
|---|---|
| 1. No<br>2. No<br>3. Yes<br>4. No<br><br>(correct response) | • understands the connections between verbal and graphical representations and can correctly interpret graphical representations of time and distance. The student understands that a verbal description of pace is the graphical equivalent to rate of change (slope) and that a faster (increased) pace is represented by a steeper rate of change (slope). [See Sample Student Response 1]<br><br>*Look for indication of the student's understanding in the written explanations of how the student got the answer.* |
| 1. Yes | • is looking at the graph as a literal picture of the verbal description. The student sees the increasing line segment as jogging uphill and the decreasing line segment as jogging downhill and does not understand the graph to be a representation of time versus distance. [See Sample Student Response 2] |
| 2. Yes | • is also looking at the graph as a literal picture but has considered the verbal references to pace. This graph incorrectly represents the steady pace as a straight line. [See Sample Student Response 3] |
| 3. No | • doesn't recognize a time versus distance graph and expects the graph to look like a literal picture of a hill. [See Sample Student Response 2] |
| 4. Yes | • is beginning to understand the relationship between time and distance but needs more experience with equating pace to rate of change (slope). Some students will answer no to this for the incorrect reason that the person is not walking downhill at the end. [See Sample Student Response 3] |

## Teaching Implications and Considerations

Ideas for eliciting more information from students about their understanding and difficulties:

- What does each of the axes represent in a time versus distance graph?
- What happens to time versus distance graphs when something or someone is getting further away? Getting closer?
- If a graph is increasing, what does it mean? If it is decreasing? If it is constant?
- Since time does not stop when a person stops walking, jogging, or running, how is this represented graphically?

Ideas for planning instruction in response to what you learned from the results of administering the Probe:

- Remind students that to show time going by, you move to the right on the graph, and to show distance getting greater, you move up on the graph. Students should understand that when distance increases on the graph, it means the person is moving away from the object and when the distance decreases on the graph, it means the person is moving closer to the object. (Van Dyke, 2002, p. 3)
- Allow students to explore time versus distance graphs with a motion detector so they connect features of the graph to the distance from (or away from) an object when a person is walking forward, backward, or staying still as time passes. This also allows students to gain an understanding of the starting point ($y$-intercept) and the walking rate (slope). There are great programs that have students "walk a given graph."
- Give students various opportunities to compare, contrast, and interpret different graphs before they are asked to draw their own. "The shift from recognizing an appropriate graph to producing a graph may be difficult for students" (Van Dyke, 2002, p. 10).
- Provide opportunities to collect actual time/distance data and represent them graphically to allow comparison of different situations.
- "Give students a graph and ask them to interpret it; give students an equation and ask them to make up a word problem for it; give students a solution and have them make up an equation or system of equations having that solution" (NCTM, 1999, p. 337).

---

## Sample Student Responses to Jogging: Graphical Representation

**Responses That Suggest Understanding**

*Sample Student Response 1*

Probe Item 1: Student chose No. If the student turned around at the top of the hill and ran slower going back down, then this one would work.

Probe Item 2: Student chose No. The person is not even moving at the beginning. They are staying still.

Probe Item 3: Student chose Yes. This one would work if the person did not turn around and go back down the hill the same way he went as the distance is still increasing. The person would be running down the back side of the hill.

Probe Item 4: Student chose No. This one is similar to #2 as the person is not moving at the beginning.

**Responses That Suggest Difficulty**

*Sample Student Response 2*

Probe Item 1: Student chose Yes. This is the only one showing anything about jogging up a hill, then jogging down.

Probe Item 3: Student chose No. The beginning is OK, but it doesn't show the person jogging downhill at the end.

*Sample Student Response 3*

Probe Item 2: Student chose Yes. This shows a steady pace (flat line), then running downhill when they are running faster.

Probe Item 4: Student chose No. The beginning part is correct as it shows a steady pace (flat line) but then it doesn't show the person running back down the hill.

## Interpreting Functions

A function is graphed below. Where is the function increasing?

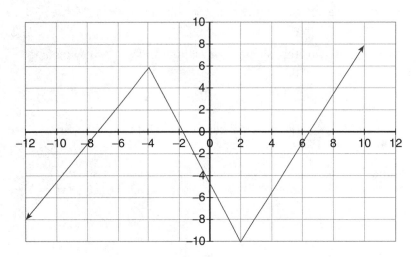

**Which choice describes where the function increasing?**

A. As the x values go from negative infinity to infinity ($-\infty < x < \infty$) the graph is always increasing.

B. The graph is increasing from negative infinity to 6 and from $-10$ to infinity ($-\infty < y < 6$ *and* $-10 < y < \infty$).

C. The graph is increasing from negative infinity to $-4$ and 2 to infinity ($-\infty < x < -4$ *and* $2 < x < \infty$).

Explain your choice:

## Teacher Notes: Interpreting Functions

### **Q**uestions to Consider About the Key Mathematical Concepts

When interpreting graphical representations of functions, do students recognize domain intervals where a function is increasing, decreasing, or constant? To what extent do they

- make sense of graphical representations?
- reason about key features of graphs?
- describe where in the domain a graph is increasing, decreasing, or constant?

---

**Common Core Connection
(CCSS.Math.Content.HSF-IF.B.4)**

**Grade:** High School

**Domain:** Functions

**Cluster:**

**Interpret functions that arise in applications in terms of the context.**

B4. For a function that models a relationship between two quantities, interpret key features of graphs and tables in terms of the quantities, and sketch graphs showing key features given a verbal description of the relationship. Key features include intercepts; intervals where the function is increasing, decreasing, positive, or negative; relative maximums and minimums; symmetries; end behavior; and periodicity.

---

### **U**ncovering Student Understanding About the Key Concepts

Using the Interpreting Functions Probe can provide the following information about how the students are thinking about key features of graphical representation.

*Do they*

- interpret the interval where a function is increasing, decreasing, or constant based on the domain (read a graph from left to right)?

OR

*Do they*

- incorrectly use the range for the interval (read a graph from top to bottom)?

*Do they*

- understand that functions other than linear functions can be increasing and decreasing?

OR

- understand that a particular function can be increasing at times and decreasing at other times?

OR

*Do they*

- see only linear functions as increasing or decreasing based on slope?

- see a function as only being able to increase or decrease?

# *E*xploring Excerpts From Educational Resources and Related Research

Areas of consideration:

Even students in advanced mathematics classes often have trouble looking at a function and deciding whether a particular interval is increasing or decreasing. (Van Dyke, 2002, p. 45)

As Schwarz and Dreyfus (1995) say, in mathematics "learning is reduced to mapping between several notation systems signifying the same abstract object." In the same paper, the authors point to the fact that research about learning functions and graphs shows persistent difficulties in linking those different notation systems. They stress that students do not succeed in tasks linking information from different settings (from a formula to a graph, even from one graph to another graph. . . .); their knowledge is compartmentalize. (Bloch, 2003, p. 6)

In the eighteenth century, when the concept of functions was developing, the idea that an expression defined on a split domain should be called a *function* was not universally accepted (Youschkevitch 1976; Kleiner 1993). . . . Although we no longer doubt the legitimacy of split domains as a function, students still have difficulty perceiving a graph having a shape like that of Euler and d'Alembert's string as the graph of a single function rather than of several joined functions (Vinner 1989). Given the centrality of the function concept in the school curriculum one cannot underestimate the importance of exposing students to this type of function. (Satianov, Fried, & Amit, 1999, p. 574)

# *S*urveying the Prompts and Selected Responses in the Probe

The Probe consists of a selected response question. The prompts and selected responses are designed to elicit understandings and common difficulties as described in the following table.

| If a student chooses | It is likely that the student |
|---|---|
| C (correct response) | • understands how to interpret or read a graph from left to right and correctly interprets features of the graph that show where a graph is increasing or decreasing. [See Sample Student Response 1]<br><br>*Look for indication of the student's understanding in the written explanations of how the student got the answer.* |
| A or B | • does not accurately interpret features of the graph that show where it is increasing or decreasing. For answer A, the student likely sees the graph as only increasing or decreasing by using the end behavior of the graph. For B, the student likely interprets the graph from top to bottom using the *y*-axis for the interval values. [See Sample Student Responses 2 and 3] |

## *T*eaching Implications and Considerations

Ideas for eliciting more information from students about their understanding and difficulties:

- Can you highlight the part of the graph that is increasing or going up? Can you highlight the part of the graph that is decreasing or going down with a different color? Can you highlight any places where it is staying constant?
- How is a graph read: left to right or top to bottom?
- When we write intervals for increasing, decreasing, or constant functions, are we describing the behavior based on how high or low it is or where on the *x*-axis it is going up, down, or horizontal?
- What part of the domain is increasing? What part of the domain is decreasing? What part of the domain is constant? Is the domain *x* values or *y* values?

Ideas for planning instruction in response to what you learned from the results of administering the Probe:

- Practice "reading" graphs from left to right. Have students come up with situations or scenarios that model different increasing, decreasing, and constant functions.
- Use a variety of functions (linear, quadratic, cubic, absolute value, piecewise, trigonometric, etc.) when discussing increasing, decreasing, or constant behavior or integrate the topic throughout the year.
- Use colored pencils or highlighters of different colors to highlight a graph where it is increasing, decreasing, or staying constant.
- Have students make marks on the *x*-axis where the graph is increasing, decreasing, or staying constant to help facilitate the use of the domain for intervals.

- When discussing increasing, decreasing, or constant behavior, talk about it as "where on the $x$-axis (domain or input values) is the graph increasing, decreasing, or staying constant" so students connect the domain and $x$-axis with the intervals.
- Use interval notation so students visually see an $x$ when describing increasing, decreasing, and constant functions.
- Relate domain with interpreting increasing, decreasing, and constant behavior.

## Sample Student Responses to Interpreting Functions

### Responses That Suggest Understanding

*Sample Student Response 1*

Probe Item C: As the values of $x$ increase, there are two increments where the $y$ values are increasing also. The $y$ values are increasing when $x$ goes from neg infinity to neg 4 and from 2 to pos infinity.

### Responses That Suggest Difficulty

*Sample Student Response 2*

Probe Item A: $x$ values are always increasing so the function is an increasing one.

*Sample Student Response 3*

Probe Item B: The lowest spot on the graph is neg infinity and that section goes to pos 6, the graph then goes down, then it increases again from neg 10 to pos infinity.

**4.3**

# Transformation of Functions

A group of students were asked how the graph of the function

$$g(x) = -2(x - 4)^2 - 7$$

was transformed from the parent function $f(x) = x^2$.

| For each group of statements, circle the statements you agree with. | Explain your choice. |
|---|---|
| **1. The graph was**<br><br>a. reflected over the *x*-axis.<br><br>b. reflected over the *y*-axis.<br><br>c. not reflected at all.<br><br>d. can't tell unless you graph it. | |
| **2. The graph was**<br><br>a. stretched horizontally.<br><br>b. stretched vertically.<br><br>c. not stretched at all.<br><br>d. can't tell unless you graph it. | |
| **3. The graph was**<br><br>a. moved to the left 4 units.<br><br>b. moved to the right 4 units.<br><br>c. moved to the left 7 units.<br><br>d. moved to the right 7 units. | |
| **4. The graph was**<br><br>a. moved up 4 units.<br><br>b. moved down 4 units.<br><br>c. moved up 7 units.<br><br>d. moved down 7 units. | |

# Teacher Notes:
# Transformation of Functions

## Questions to Consider About the Key Mathematical Concepts

When working with functions, do students understand how algebraic representations describe graphical transformations? To what extent do they

- make sense of various forms of algebraic representations and correctly relate them to a graphical transformation?
- reason about the correspondences between algebraic and graphical representations?
- describe graphical effects of various algebraic transformations?

## Common Core Connection
## (CCSS.Math.Content.HSF-BF.B.3)

**Grade:** High School

**Domain:** Functions

**Cluster:**

**Build new functions from existing functions.**

B3. Identify the effect on the graph of replacing $f(x)$ by $f(x) + k$, $k\,f(x)$, $f(kx)$, and $f(x + k)$ for specific values of $k$ (both positive and negative); find the value of $k$ given the graphs. Experiment with cases and illustrate an explanation of the effects on the graph using technology. Include recognizing even and odd functions from their graphs and algebraic expressions for them.

## Uncovering Student Understanding About the Key Concepts

Using the Transformation of Functions Probe can provide the following information about how the students are thinking about algebraic and graphical transformations.

*Do they*

- recognize a horizontal or vertical translation and/or stretch?

OR

*Do they*

- not recognize the placement of the numbers as a clue as to the type of translation?

*Do they*

- correctly apply the direction of a translation using the opposite sign for the horizontal translation and the same sign for the vertical translation?

OR

- understand that multiplying by a negative number "flips" the graph?

OR

*Do they*

- apply an incorrect direction to the horizontal and/or vertical translation ?

- only see the negative as part of the number that will stretch or compress the graph?

## Exploring Excerpts From Educational Resources and Related Research

Areas of consideration:

The concept of function transformations is a central theme from algebra through calculus, yet it is one that many students fail to internalize. (Poetzel et al., 2012, p. 103)

Students may find the effect of adding a constant to the input variable to be counterintuitive, because the effect on the graph appears to be the opposite to the transformation on the variable, e.g., the graph of $y = f(x + 2)$ is a horizontal translation of the graph of $y = f(x) - 2$ units along the $x$-axis rather than in the opposite direction. (Common Core Standards Writing Team, 2013b)

When a problem involves a function which can be the result of the application of a set of transformations on a basic function, students are generally able to identify some of the transformations that have been applied. Students who had difficulties with this type of tasks found troublesome to associate a function represented graphically with its corresponding analytical representation. They showed a tendency to use memorized facts or to make a table of data in order to succeed in these tasks. . . . A smaller group of students showed a tendency to generalize the conservation of distance property, which is valid for rigid transformations, to non-rigid transformations, demonstrating that they apply actions or processes to the graph of the function as if it was a rigid object, with no reflection on what the result of those actions would be for each particular point on the domain of the function. . . . In questions related to rigid transformations, students had more difficulties recognizing a horizontal translation than a vertical translation. This seems to be due to the fact that students memorize the rules for transformations and their corresponding effect on the function. When remembering this information students often associate the incorrect direction to the translation. (Alatorre et al., 2006, pp. 26–27)

## Surveying the Prompts and Selected Responses in the Probe

The Probe consists of four separate selected response items. The prompts and selected responses are designed to elicit understandings and common difficulties as described below:

| If a student chooses | It is likely that the student |
|---|---|
| 1. a, 2. b, 3. b, 4. d (correct responses) | • recognizes graphical transformations based on algebraic representations. [See Sample Student Response 1]<br><br>*Look for indication of the student's understanding in the written explanations of how the student got the answer.* |
| Various other response patterns | • fails to recognize various features of algebraic representations that show graphical transformation. Often this has to do with an error in direction of a translation (Questions 3 and 4) or how a function is vertically or horizontally stretched or compressed (Question 2). [See Sample Student Responses 2, 3, 4, and 5] |

## Teaching Implications and Considerations

Ideas for eliciting more information from students about their understanding and difficulties:

- What is the parent function? What does the parent function look like? What are some key features of the parent function?
- What does each number in the transformation function tell you about the graph?
- What do the different signs (positive or negative) tell you about a transformation? Can you give an example of a number that would translate a function to the right 3 units? To the left 3 units? Up 3 units? Down 3 units?
- Can you graph this function and describe the transformation from its parent function? Can you explain how the graph correlates to the equation (algebraic representation)?

Ideas for planning instruction in response to what you learned from the results of administering the Probe:

- The use of technology to introduce transformations is a powerful tool for making connections between parent and transformed functions. Explore individual transformations from a parent function one at a time to highlight the effect of each transformation,. Let them "see" what the numbers in the algebraic representation "do" to the graph.
- When working with equations, show students that the number that describes a vertical translation can be moved to the side with the $y$ variable. This helps students understand that the opposite sign of

this number is also used just like with the number near the $x$ variable that describes a horizontal translation (write $y = -2(x - 4)^2 - 7$ as $y + 7 = -2(x - 4)^2$). By moving the 7 to the other side of the equation, the opposite sign is already being accounted for.

- Allow students to explore various types of functions (linear, quadratic, square root, absolute value, cubic, piecewise, trigonometric, etc.). This allows students to see how the transformation "rules" apply to all functions.
- Integrate the study of transformations throughout the study of functions, starting with linear and moving to higher order functions.

## Sample Student Responses to Transformation of Functions

### Responses That Suggest Understanding

*Sample Student Response 1*

Probe Item 1: Student chose a. Because of the leading negative, the graph is reflected over the $x$-axis (flipped).

Probe Item 2: Student chose b. The number in front of the parenthesis is greater than 1; this graph grows faster than the parent function and therefore is stretched vertically.

Probe Item 3: Student chose b. The −4 is what moves the graph horizontally as it is with the $x$ value. It moves in the opposite direction, therefore in the positive direction (right) 4 units.

Probe Item 4: Student chose d. The −7 is what moves the graph vertically. It was originally with the $y$ value as a +7, and we have already taken the opposite value by moving it to the right side; therefore, it would move it up 7 units.

### Responses That Suggest Difficulty

*Sample Student Response 2*

Probe Item 1: Student chose d. Without graphing this, we cannot tell if it is reflected or not. Put it into a graphing calculator to see.

*Sample Student Response 3*

Probe Item 2: Student chose d. The 2 makes it more narrow, I think, but I am not sure if it stretches it or not.

*Sample Student Response 4*

Probe Item 3: Student chose a. The neg 4 moves it left or right and neg is to the left, so left 4 units would be the right answer.

*Sample Student Response 5*

Probe Item 4: Student chose c. The 7 moves the graph up or down, and we need to take the opposite sign. This would mean in the positive direction (up) 7 units.

**Variation: Transformation of Functions—Trig**

How is the graph of the sine function

$$g(x) = \frac{1}{2} \sin \left(4x - \frac{\pi}{3}\right) + 5$$

transformed from the parent function $f(x) = \sin x$?

| For each group of statements, circle the statement you agree with. | Explain your choice. |
|---|---|
| 1. The amplitude of $g(x)$ is<br><br>a. $\frac{1}{2}$<br><br>b. 1<br><br>c. 4<br><br>d. 5 | |
| 2. The period of $g(x)$ is<br><br>a. $\frac{\pi}{3}$<br><br>b. $\frac{\pi}{2}$<br><br>c. $\frac{1}{2}$<br><br>d. Can't tell unless you graph it | |
| 3. The graph of $g(x)$ has a<br><br>a. Phase shift of $-\frac{\pi}{3}$<br>b. Phase shift of $-\frac{\pi}{12}$<br>c. Phase shift of 2<br>d. Phase shift of $\frac{1}{2}$<br>e. Can't tell unless you graph it | |
| 4. The graph was<br><br>a. Shifted down $\frac{\pi}{3}$ units<br>b. Shifted up 4 units<br>c. Shifted up 5 units<br>d. Shifted up $\frac{1}{2}$ unit<br>e. Can't tell unless you graph it | |

## Circular Measurement

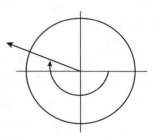

| Determine whether each measure is an accurate estimate for the angle created by the arc drawn on the circle. | | | | |

---

**A. 150°**          Circle one:     Yes      No      Can't determine

Explain your choice:

---

**B. –210°**          Circle one:     Yes      No      Can't determine

Explain your choice:

---

**C. $\frac{\pi}{3}$**          Circle one:     Yes      No      Can't determine

Explain your choice:

---

**D. $\frac{-2\pi}{3}$**          Circle one:     Yes      No      Can't determine

Explain your choice:

---

**E. $\frac{-7\pi}{6}$**          Circle one:     Yes      No      Can't determine

Explain your choice:

# Teacher Notes:
# Circular Measurement

## **Q**uestions to Consider About the Key Mathematical Concepts

When solving problems with circular measurements, can students accurately determine an estimate for the measure of an arc drawn in a circle? To what extent do they

- make sense of direction and magnitude in a circle?
- reason about degree and radian measures?
- describe the direction and estimated measure of the angle drawn?

---

### **Common Core Connection (CCSS.Math.Content.HSF-TF.A.1; CCSS.Math.Content.HSF-TF.A.2)**

**Grade:** High School

**Domain:** Functions

**Cluster:**

**Extend the domain of trigonometric functions using the unit circle.**

A1. Understand radian measure of an angle as the length of the arc on the unit circle subtended by the angle.

A2. Explain how the unit circle in the coordinate plane enables the extension of trigonometric functions to all real numbers, interpreted as radian measures of angles traversed counterclockwise around the unit circle.

---

## **U**ncovering Student Understanding About the Key Concepts

Using the Circular Measurement Probe can provide the following information about how the students are thinking about angle measures in the unit circle.

*Do they*

- recognize the direction of an angle drawn in the unit circle?

OR

*Do they*

- assume all angles are positive, or confuse the directions of a positive angle?

- understand degree measure in a unit circle to be 360°?

OR

- misunderstand it to be something other than 360°?

*Do they*

- understand radian measure in a unit circle to be 2π?

OR

- understand 180° and π represent the same magnitude but not the same value?

OR

- correctly divide the circle (or semicircle) into increments when using radian measure (ex: dividing π in thirds would make six sections in the whole circle)?

OR

*Do they*

- confuse the radian measure of a complete circle (2π) with being one turn so it is π?

- see 180° equal to π (same value)?

- incorrectly divide the circle (or semicircle) using the whole circle as π instead of 2π (ex: incorrectly dividing π in thirds to make three sections in the whole circle instead of six)?

## *E*xploring Excerpts From Educational Resources and Related Research

Areas of consideration:

While the unit circle is a central concept of trigonometry, students' and teachers' understandings of trigonometric functions typically lack connections to the unit circle. Pre-service and in-service teachers often hold limited and fragmented understandings of central trigonometry concepts (Akkoc, 2008; Fi, 2006; Thompson, Carlson, & Silverman, 2007; Topçu, Kertil, Akkoç, Yilmaz, & Önder, 2006). Given that teachers have shallow understandings of trigonometry, it should come as no surprise that students construct disconnected understandings of trigonometric functions and topics foundational to trigonometry (Brown, 2006; Weber, 2005). (Moore, LaForest & Kim, 2012, p. 16)

Trigonometry is an important subject in the high school mathematics curriculum. As one of the secondary mathematics topics that are taught early and that link algebraic, geometric, and graphical reasoning, trigonometry can serve as an important precursor to calculus as well as college level courses relating to Newtonian physics, architecture, surveying, and engineering. Unfortunately, many high school students are not accustomed to these types of reasoning (Blackett and Tall 1991), and learning about trigonometric functions is initially fraught with difficulty. Trigonometry presents many first-time challenges for students: It requires students to relate diagrams of triangles to numerical relationships and manipulate the symbols involved in such relationships. Further, trigonometric functions are typically among the first functions that students cannot evaluate directly by performing arithmetic operations. (Weber, 2008, p. 144)

## Surveying the Prompts and Selected Responses in the Probe

The Probe consists of five selected response items, each related to a common figure. The prompts and selected responses are designed to elicit understandings and common difficulties as described below:

| *If a student chooses* | *It is likely that the student* |
|---|---|
| A. No, B. Yes, C. No, D. No, and E. Yes (correct responses) | • understands angle measurement in the unit circle using degrees (B) and radians (E). The direction of the drawn angle is clockwise; therefore, the angle is negative. It goes beyond 180° ($\pi$ radians), so the only two possibilities would be choices B and E. [See Sample Student Response 1]<br><br>*Look for indication of the student's understanding in the written explanations of how the student got the answer.* |
| A. Yes and D. Yes | • does not recognize the direction of the angle being drawn as representing a negative angle. Often students ignore the direction given for an angle and base the angle measure on the location of the terminating side. Other students incorrectly represent a positive angle with a clockwise rotation and a negative angle with a counterclockwise rotation. [See Sample Student Responses 2 and 3] |
| C. Yes and D. Yes | • is incorrectly looking at the radian measure of a whole circle as $\pi$ instead of the semicircle as $\pi$. The student is probably splitting up the whole circle into thirds instead of half the circle into thirds. [See Sample Student Responses 3 and 4] |

## Teaching Implications and Considerations

Ideas for eliciting more information from students about their understanding and difficulties:

- What direction is the angle being drawn? How do you know?
- What is the sign of an angle drawn clockwise? Counterclockwise?
- How many degrees in a circle? In a semicircle?
- What is the radian measure of a circle? Of a semicircle?
- How many sections are in a circle if each $\pi$ radians is divided into thirds? How many sections are in a circle if each 180° are divided into thirds? How about fourths? Sixths?
- How many degrees in a radian? How many radians in a degree?

Ideas for planning instruction in response to what you learned from the results of administering the Probe:

- Give students many opportunities to explore angles in the unit circle, using both degree and radian measures. Draw angles in different quadrants and different directions and use measures above 360° (2π radians).
- Use technology or tools such as Trig Trainers to explore angle measures.
- Although we often use the unit circle as it is helpful in creating graphs of trigonometric functions, allow students to explore circles with radii other than 1.

## Sample Student Responses to Circular Measurement

### Responses That Suggest Understanding

*Sample Student Response 1*

Probe Item A: Student chose No. The arrow shows a negative angle (clockwise). This would be correct if the arrow was going counterclockwise.

Probe Item B: Student chose Yes. The arrow is showing a negative turn and it goes past −180° a little so −210° would be a good estimate.

Probe Item C: Student chose No. Wrong direction. Plus $\frac{\pi}{3}$ is not in that area anyway.

Probe Item D: Student chose No. The negative is correct but $-\frac{2\pi}{3}$ would be in the third quadrant.

Probe Item E: Student chose Yes. The negative means clockwise, which is correct. $\frac{6\pi}{6}$ would be 1π, which is halfway around the circle as a full circle is 2π. It goes just a little further, so it is a good estimate.

### Responses That Suggest Difficulty

*Sample Student Response 2*

Probe Item A: Student chose Yes. Halfway around would be 180°, and backing it up a bit would be around 150°.

Probe Item B: Student chose No. Halfway is 180°, so 210° would be even further past the halfway point.

*Sample Student Response 3*

Probe Item C: Student chose Yes. If I were to split the circle into thirds, the line would be about a third of the circle.

Probe Item D: Student chose No. It is way under $\frac{2}{3}$ of the circle.

Probe Item E: Student chose No. $\frac{7}{6}$ is over a whole circle.

*Sample Student Response 4*

Probe Item D: Student chose Yes. Negative means clockwise, and it is about $\frac{2}{3}$ of the way around the circle going clockwise.

## Direct and Inverse Variation

Determine whether each of the following represents direct or inverse variation.

| Circle the correct answer. | Explain your choice. |
|---|---|
| **1.** <br> a. Direct variation <br> b. Inverse variation <br> c. Neither <br> d. Not enough information to determine | |
| **2.** $$y = -\frac{3}{5}x$$ <br> a. Direct variation <br> b. Inverse variation <br> c. Neither <br> d. Not enough information to determine | |
| **3.** <br> a. Direct variation <br> b. Inverse variation <br> c. Neither <br> d. Not enough information to determine | |

| Circle the correct answer. | Explain your choice. |
|---|---|
| **4.** $$y = \frac{3}{x}$$ a. Direct variation<br>b. Inverse variation<br>c. Neither<br>d. Not enough information to determine | |
| **5.** 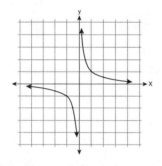 a. Direct variation<br>b. Inverse variation<br>c. Neither<br>d. Not enough information to determine | |
| **6.** $$y = -\frac{2}{3}x + 5$$ a. Direct variation<br>b. Inverse variation<br>c. Neither<br>d. Not enough information to determine | |

# Teacher Notes:
# Direct and Inverse Variation

## Questions to Consider About the Key Mathematical Concepts

Can students distinguish between examples and nonexamples of direct and inverse relationships? To what extent do they

- understand direct variation as a situation where two quantities are related in such a way that the ratio of their values always remains constant?
- understand inverse variation as a situation in which one quantity increases while another quantity decreases (i.e., if $b$ is inversely proportional to $a$, the equation is of the form $b = k/a$)?
- make sense of directly and inversely related data in various forms?
- describe characteristics of direct and inverse relationships in their justifications?

### Common Core Connection
### (CCSS.Math.Content.HSF-LE.A.1b)

**Grade:** High School

**Domain:** Functions

**Cluster:**

**Construct and compare linear, quadratic, and exponential models and solve problems.**

A1b. Recognize situations in which one quantity changes at a constant rate per unit interval relative to another.

## Uncovering Student Understanding About the Key Concepts

Using the Direct and Inverse Variation Probe can provide the following information about how the students are thinking about direct and inverse variation.

*Do they*
- recognize the characteristics of direct variation?

OR

*Do they*
- describe all lines as direct variation and all "curves" as inverse?
- describe only equations with positive $k$ values as direct variation?

- recognize the characteristics of inverse variation?

OR

- confuse negative $k$ values with inverse variation?

## Exploring Excerpts From Educational Resources and Related Research

Areas of consideration:

Swafford and Langrall (2000) noted that inverse variation situation is the most difficult for students due to the lack of understanding about the concept of inverse variation. It was suggested that students need more exploration with this situation before studying them analytically in algebra. Thus, in this study, the inverse variation tasks represent various stages. That is, initially the ability to solve the numerical examples and later the ability to use the algebraic method. In other words, they should be able to find the answers by performing numerical operation on given values of the independent variable before applying the algebraic symbol to represent the situation. (Lim Hooi & Wun Thiam, 2012, p. 180)

## Surveying the Prompts and Selected Responses in the Probe

The Probe consists of six selected response items. The prompts and selected responses are designed to elicit understandings and common difficulties as described below:

| If a student chooses | It is likely that the student |
|---|---|
| 1. a, 2. a, 3. c, 4. b, 5. b, 6. c (correct responses) | • recognizes the differences between direct variation, inverse variation, linear, and quadratic relationships. [See Sample Student Response 1] <br><br> *Look for indication of the student's understanding in the written explanations of how the student got the answer.* |
| 2. b, 4. a, 6. b | • is associating a *negative k* value with inverse variation. [See Sample Student Response 2] |
| 3. b | • is associating "curved" graphs with inverse variation. [See Sample Student Response 3] |
| 6. a | • is associating linear graphs with direct variation. [See Sample Student Response 4] |

## Teaching Implications and Considerations

Ideas for eliciting more information from students about their understanding and difficulties:

- What are some characteristics of direct variation? Inverse variation?
- How does direct variation relate to linear relationships?
- How does inverse variation differ from quadratic relationships?
- How is direct variation shown as an equation? As a graph?
- How is inverse variation shown as an equation? As a graph?

Ideas for planning instruction in response to what you learned from the results of administering the Probe:

- Use technology as an avenue for students to make connections between the graphs of equations and their algebraic representations.
- Provide multiple opportunities for students to work within a context for direct and inverse variation.
- Use examples and nonexamples in all forms: contexts, tables, graphs, and equations.
- Use the vocabulary of direct and inverse variation whenever it applies so students get used to hearing the terms and connecting the ideas to multiple examples.

## Sample Student Responses to Direct and Inverse Variation

### Responses That Suggest Understanding

*Sample Student Response 1*

Probe Item 1: Student chose a. I know direct variation is same as proportional and this is a graph of proportional relationship.

Probe Item 2: Student chose a. This is an equation for a proportional relationship so not an example of inverse.

Probe Item 3: Student chose c. This is a parabola, so not direct or inverse.

Probe Item 4: Student chose b. This equation shows inverse because $x * y = 3$.

Probe Item 5: Student chose b. We have graphed a lot of these in the calculator, so I know this as inverse. I checked examples by labeling the graph by 1s and checking values of $x$ and $y$.

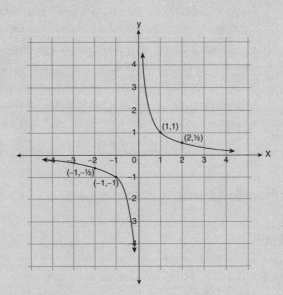

Probe Item 6: Student chose c. This is linear, but because of the +5, it isn't direct.

**Responses That Suggest Difficulty**

*Sample Student Response 2*

Probe Item 2: Student chose b. With (−) in front of the $\frac{3}{5}$, the line goes to the left so would be considered inverse.

*Sample Student Response 3*

Probe Item 3: Student chose b. Sometimes you get straight lines when you graph equations, and sometimes you get curved lines. Straight is direct, and not straight is inverse.

*Sample Student Response 4*

Probe Item 6: Student chose a. This equation is a line when you graph it, and all lines are examples of direct variation.

## Variation: Direct and Inverse Card Sort

| Inverse Variation | NOT<br>Inverse Variation |
|---|---|
| **A.** 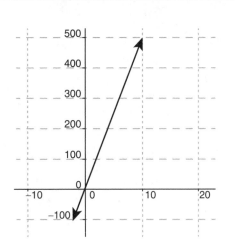 | **B.** 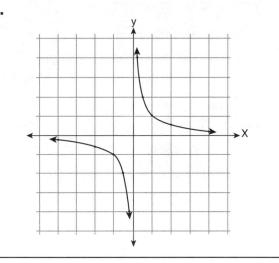 |
| **C.** $$y = -\frac{3}{5}x$$ | **D.** <br>| $x$ | $y$ |<br>\|---\|---\|<br>\| 1 \| 2 \|<br>\| 2 \| 1 \|<br>\| 3 \| $\frac{2}{3}$ \|<br>\| 4 \| $\frac{1}{2}$ \| |
| **E.** 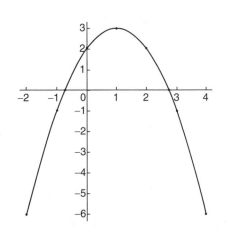 | **F.** $$y = \frac{3}{x}$$ |

| Inverse Variation | NOT<br>Inverse Variation |
|---|---|
| **G.**<br><br>| x | y |<br>|---|---|<br>| −1 | 30 |<br>| −2 | 40 |<br>| −3 | 50 |<br>| −4 | 60 | | **H.**<br> |
| **I.**<br><br>$$xy = -8$$ | **J.**<br><br>$$y = -\frac{2}{3}x + 5$$ |

## Equation of the Function

4.6

Determine whether each equation could represent the graph of the following function.

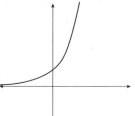

**A.** $y = x^2 + 5$     Circle one:    Yes    No    Can't determine

Explain your choice:

**B.** $y = 2.5^x$     Circle one:    Yes    No    Can't determine

Explain your choice:

**C.** $y = 4x + 5$     Circle one:    Yes    No    Can't determine

Explain your choice:

**D.** $y = 10^x$     Circle one:    Yes    No    Can't determine

Explain your choice:

**E.** $y = 4x^2$     Circle one:    Yes    No    Can't determine

Explain your choice:

# Teacher Notes:
# Equation of the Function

## **Q**uestions to Consider About the Key Mathematical Concepts

When given a graph of an exponential function without labeled intervals, can students determine possible algebraic representations of the graph? To what extent do they

- make sense of information given in graphical and symbolic forms?
- describe the features of exponential functions that allow them to determine whether different representations are equivalent?
- distinguish between linear, exponential, and quadratic functions?

### Common Core Connection
### (CCSS.Math.Content.HSF-LE.A.2)

**Grade:** High School

**Domain:** Functions

**Cluster:**

**Construct and compare linear, quadratic, and exponential models and solve problems.**

A2. Construct linear and exponential functions, including arithmetic and geometric sequences, given a graph, a description of a relationship, or two input-output pairs (include reading these from a table).

## **U**ncovering Student Understanding About the Key Concepts

Using the Equation of the Function Probe can provide the following information about how the students are thinking about multiple representations of exponential functions.

*Do they*

- look for relevant information shown in the graph that will help determine possible equations (increasing "rate of change" and *y*-intercept)?

OR

*Do they*

- not see the relationship between a graph and its equation?

| *Do they* | | *Do they* | |
| --- | --- | --- | --- |
| • recognize key features of exponential functions when written in algebraic form? | OR | • not differentiate between $b^x$ versus $x^b$? | |
| • consider how the sizes of the intervals would change the appearance of the function? | OR | • make choices based on the assumption the intervals are 1 unit? | |

## Exploring Excerpts From Educational Resources and Related Research

Areas of consideration:

Students fail to recognize the underlying equivalence when the same set of points is represented by a graph or an equation or a table. They tend to see changes in form as producing unrelated representations. (NCTM, 1999, p. 215)

Students may not see the links between different representations of a functional relation—for example, the mutual dependence between a function's graph and equation, or between its table and equation. (Driscoll, 1999, p. 146)

## Surveying the Prompts and Selected Responses in the Probe

The Probe consists of five selected response items each relating to a common graph. The prompts and selected responses are designed to elicit understandings and common difficulties as described below:

| *If a student chooses* | *It is likely that the student* |
| --- | --- |
| A. No, B. Yes, C. No, D. Yes, and E. No (correct responses) | • recognizes the graph represents an exponential function and that, depending on the interval, both B and D are possible symbolic representations for exponential functions. [See Sample Student Response 1]<br><br>*Look for indication of the student's understanding in the written explanations of how the student got the answer.* |

| If a student chooses | It is likely that the student |
|---|---|
| Various other patterns | • fails to recognize one or more of the following key features of equations and graphs that link them together as representing the same information:<br><br>  o any equation that includes an exponent is exponential [See Sample Student Response 2]<br>  o eliminates $y = 10^x$ [See Sample Student Response 3]<br>  o various other incorrect ideas [See Sample Student Response 4] |

## Teaching Implications and Considerations

Ideas for eliciting more information from students about their understanding and difficulties:

- Is the graph linear, quadratic, or exponential? How can you tell?
- What information can be obtained from the graph that can help determine a possible equation?
- What are some key features of the equations that might help to graph them?
- What do the numbers in the equation represent ?
- Are the equations linear, quadratic, or exponential? How can you tell?
- Where does the graph cross the $y$-axis? What could the $y$ value be at this point given different interval possibilities?

Ideas for planning instruction in response to what you learned from the results of administering the Probe:

- Use technology as an avenue for students to make connections between the different types of representations and to analyze results of changes in sizes of intervals.
- Focus students on key features of various types of functions and their related graphs.
- Allow students ample opportunities to explore the explicit connections between and solve problems in which they use, tables, graphs, words, and symbolic representations.
- "Students should see algebra not just as the process of transforming and manipulating symbols but rather as a tool for expressing and analyzing relationships between quantities that change" (NCTM, 1999, p. 215).
- Have students explore the advantages and disadvantages of representing a relationship with each of the different types of representation.

## Sample Student Responses to Equation of the Function

**Responses That Suggest Understanding**

*Sample Student Response 1*

Probe Item A: Student chose No. This would be a parabola.

Probe Item B: Student chose Yes. This is an exponential graph that would have an equation with a positive *y*-intercept and would look like this. You would never get a negative *y* because *x* is an exponent.

Probe Item C: Student chose No. The graph of this equation would be a straight line.

Probe Item D: Student chose Yes. Same as what I said for B.

Probe Item E: Student chose No. Same as what I said for A.

**Responses That Suggest Difficulty**

*Sample Student Response 2*

Probe Item A: Student chose Yes. Equations with powers have curvy graphs.

*Sample Student Response 3*

Probe Item D: Student chose No. The 10 seems too big to me even though the *x* is in the right spot.

*Sample Student Response 4*

Probe Item C: Student chose Yes. 4 is positive and this is going up to the right. The *b* is positive and this graph is crossing the *x*-axis at a positive number.

## Variation: Equation of the Function

Determine whether each equation could represent the graph of the following function.

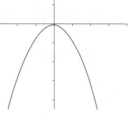

**A.** $y = 3x^2 - 5$    Circle one:    Yes    No    Can't determine

Explain your choice:

**B.** $y = -4^x$    Circle one:    Yes    No    Can't determine

Explain your choice:

**C.** $y = -3x^2 - 5x - 6$    Circle one:    Yes    No    Can't determine

Explain your choice:

**D.** $y = 10^x$    Circle one:    Yes    No    Can't determine

Explain your choice:

**E.** $y = -4x^2$    Circle one:    Yes    No    Can't determine

Explain your choice:

## Logarithms

| Given the following information, which of the following are true? |
| --- |

$$\log_{10} y = x \ \text{ and } \ x < 0$$

Explain your reasoning on each choice.

---

**A.** $y < 0$      Circle one:     Sometimes     Always     Never

Explain your choice:

---

**B.** $y = 0$      Circle one:     Sometimes     Always     Never

Explain your choice:

---

**C.** $0 < y < 1$      Circle one:     Sometimes     Always     Never

Explain your choice:

---

**D.** $y > 10$      Circle one:     Sometimes     Always     Never

Explain your choice:

## Teacher Notes: Logarithms

## **Q**uestions to Consider About the Key Mathematical Concepts

When analyzing logarithms, do students understand how to evaluate a logarithm by first expressing it as an exponential equation? To what extent do they

- make sense of the relationship between logarithmic and exponential functions?
- reason that rewriting a logarithm in exponential form will allow numbers or unknowns to be evaluated or analyzed?
- describe or show how a logarithm can be written in exponential form?

### Common Core Connection (CCSS.Math.Content.HSF-LE.A.4; CCSS.Math.Content.HSF-BF.B.5)

**Grade:** High School

**Domain:** Functions

**Cluster:**

**Construct and compare linear, quadratic, and exponential models and solve problems.**

A4. For exponential models, express as a logarithm the solution to $ab^{ct} = d$, where $a$, $c$, and $d$ are numbers and the base $b$ is 2, 10, or $e$; evaluate the logarithm using technology.

**Cluster:**

**Build new functions from existing functions.**

B5. Understand the inverse relationship between exponents and logarithms and use this relationship to solve problems involving logarithms and exponents.

## **U**ncovering Student Understanding About the Key Concepts

Using the Logarithms Probe can provide the following information about how the students are thinking about the connections between logarithmic and exponential functions.

*Do they*

- understand the relationship between logarithmic and exponential functions?

OR

- understand that a log is an exponent (a number)?

OR

- rewrite the equation as $10^x = y$, then reason that because $x$ is negative, $10^x$ can be moved to the denominator to make it positive?

OR

- reason about what values of $y$ would make the equation true?

OR

*Do they*

- see the two types of functions as unrelated?

- see "log" as a variable instead of an operator?

- try to solve the equation as is or with a calculator?

- see too many variables and believe it is unsolvable?

# Exploring Excerpts From Educational Resources and Related Research

Areas of consideration:

Anecdotal evidence from both students and teachers over the years has consistently shown that the topic of logarithms is one of the most abstract units to learn, and teach as well, in secondary schools. Even though students can often perform the tasks that are given in the text and during the examinations, their understanding of the fundamental concept of logarithms still remains in doubt. (Chua, 2003, intro)

The results of this study appear to point to a lack of a good understanding of logarithms among students, in particular, the failure to perceive the logarithm as an exponent, and hence a number. . . . New notations are often difficult for students, and they should therefore be firmly established at the start. In the case of [log] notation, students often perceive [log] as a variable, rather than an operator because of its resemblance to algebraic notations with which they are familiar. (Chua, 2003, pp. 4, 5)

The applications of logarithms can be confounding to students because logs appear in a somewhat mysterious and less familiar kind of notation. As mathematics instruction slowly transitions from the "how" to the "why," we are able to observe students' discomfort with logarithm-based questions that require more than procedural fluency, such as those relating to compound interest on a bank account or calculating the intensity of an earthquake. From a typical chapter on logarithms, students are expected to apply the rules of logs, expand or condense algebraic expressions involving logarithms, and solve equations involving logarithms. Students are also often instructed that logarithms represent exponents and that the logarithm notation denotes the inverse of an exponential function. But even if students can conquer mechanical fluency, many still are confused about what all the procedures really mean and how the logarithm concepts can be recognized and applied in more advanced mathematics or in other disciplines such as physics, biology, or chemistry. (Ostler, 2013, p. 670)

## Surveying the Prompts and Selected Responses in the Probe

The Probe consists of four selected response items, each related to a common figure. The prompts and selected responses are designed to elicit understandings and common difficulties as described below:

| If a student chooses | It is likely that the student |
|---|---|
| A. Never, B. Never, C. Always, and D. Never (correct responses) | • understands how to evaluate a logarithmic function by first expressing it as an exponential function. $Log_{10} y = x$ can be written as $10^x = y$. When $x < 0$, then $10^x$ can be written as $\dfrac{1}{10^x}$ to allow $x$ to be positive and $y$ to be evaluated. [See Sample Student Response 1] <br><br> *Look for indication of the student's understanding in the written explanations of how the student got the answer.* |
| A. Sometimes or always | • either does not have an understanding of logarithms and/or how to write them as exponential functions or thinks that a number raised to a negative power to be equivalent to a negative number. [See Sample Student Responses 2 and 3] |
| B. Sometimes or always | • does not have an understanding of logarithms and/or how to write them as exponential functions. [See Sample Student Response 3] |
| D. Sometimes or always | • either does not have an understanding of logarithms and/or how to write them as exponential functions or thinks that 10 raised to any power will be a number greater than 10. [See Sample Student Responses 2 and 3] |

## Teaching Implications and Considerations

Ideas for eliciting more information from students about their understanding and difficulties:

- Read "$log_{10} 100 = x$" (log to the base 10 of 100 is equal to what). What does this mean? (The exponent required on base 10 to give the value 100)
- What does "$log_3 27 = x$" mean? (The exponent required on base 3 to give the value of 27)

- Read "$\log_{10} y = x$" (log to the base 10 of $y$ is equal to what). What does this mean? (The exponent required on base 10 to give the value of $y$)
- If $x$ is less than 0, what are some possible numbers $x$ could be?
- If a number is raised to a negative number, what does it mean? If 10 is raised to a negative number, what does that mean?
- How can you rewrite the functions so the negative exponents are positive?

Ideas for planning instruction in response to what you learned from the results of administering the Probe:

- As logarithmic functions are usually a new area of study for students, allow them ample time to explore the equations and graphs.
- "It is important for students not only to be able to evaluate terms like $\log_2 8$ or $\log_5 25$, but also understand what they mean as well. So when introducing the topic of logarithms, a good teaching strategy is to spend some time at the start to have students first articulate the logarithmic expression and then explain its meaning before evaluating it. For example, when $\log_2 8$ is given, get them to read it as 'log to the base 2 of 8' and then give its meaning as 'the exponent required on the base 2 to give the value 8'. This helps them to evaluate the expression easily to give 3. In doing so, an attempt is made to get them to see that the expression $\log_2 8$ is not merely made up of three separate entities but rather a single numerical value which turns out to be an exponent. To reinforce the concept of a logarithm as an exponent, teachers can encourage students to evaluate expressions like $\log_4 2$ and $\log_2 \frac{1}{4}$" (Chua, 2003, p. 4).
- Help students to understand "log" is not a variable that one can divide by to "get rid of." If students have studied units on trigonometry, compare the word *log* with *sin*, *cos*, and *tan*.
- Show students graphically how logarithmic and exponential functions are inverses of each other.
- Introduce logs after a unit on exponential functions, especially if the students have an understanding of inverse functions.
- Explore the usefulness of logs as a tool to solve exponential equations that would otherwise be very difficult to solve.

## Sample Student Responses to Logarithms

### Responses That Suggest Understanding

*Sample Student Response 1*

Probe Item C: Student chose Always. $\log_{10} y = x$ can be rewritten as $10^x = y$. If $x < 0$, then it is a negative number. 10 raised to a negative number would be a very small positive number as the negative would move the 10 into the denominator ($1/10^x$). This means that answers A ($y < 0$), B ($y = 0$), and D ($y > 10$) could never be true.

**Responses That Suggest Difficulty**

*Sample Student Response 2*

Probe Item A: Student chose Always. If *x* is less than 0, then *y* would have to be less than 0 too.

Probe Item D: Student chose Always. If 10 is raised to a power, then it would have to be bigger than it started.

*Sample Student Response 3*

Probe Items A–D: Student chose Sometimes. We would need more information about the numbers to say always or never.

# 5

# Geometry Probes

The content of the Probes in this chapter aligns with the standards for high school but is often taught in different courses across districts. The Probes and their variations are also relevant beyond the aligned course level for students in more advanced courses who have not yet met particular standards from previous courses as well as for students who have already met the standards in the current course.

We developed these Probes to address this critical area of focus for high school students, described in the standards (Council of Chief State School Officers [CCSSO], 2010) as follows:

- Prove theorems about lines and angles. *Theorems include the following: Vertical angles are congruent; when a transversal crosses parallel lines, alternate interior angles are congruent and corresponding angles are congruent; and points on a perpendicular bisector of a line segment are exactly those equidistant from the segment's endpoints.*
- Prove theorems about triangles. *Theorems include the following: Measures of interior angles of a triangle sum to 180°, base angles of isosceles triangles are congruent, the segment joining midpoints of two sides of a triangle is parallel to the third side and half the length, and the medians of a triangle meet at a point.*
- Prove theorems about parallelograms. *Theorems include the following: Opposite sides are congruent, opposite angles are congruent, the diagonals of a parallelogram bisect each other, and, conversely, rectangles are parallelograms with congruent diagonals.*
- Identify the shapes of two-dimensional cross sections of three-dimensional objects, and identify three-dimensional objects generated by rotations of two-dimensional objects.

- Identify and describe relationships among inscribed angles, radii, and chords. *Include the relationship between central, inscribed, and circumscribed angles; inscribed angles on a diameter are right angles; the radius of a circle is perpendicular to the tangent where the radius intersects the circle.*
- Use trigonometric ratios and the Pythagorean theorem to solve right triangles in applied problems.
- Use volume formulas for cylinders, pyramids, cones, and spheres to solve problems.
- Use trigonometric ratios and the Pythagorean theorem to solve right triangles in applied problems.

> The content of the Probes in this chapter aligns with the standards for high school but is often taught in different courses across districts. The Probes and their variations are also relevant beyond the aligned course level for students in more advanced courses who have not yet met particular standards from previous courses as well as for students who have already met the standards in the current course.

The standards and their related questions, as well as the Probes associated with them, are shown in Table 5.1.

**Table 5.1**  Geometry Probes

| Common Core Mathematical Content | Related Question | Probe Name |
|---|---|---|
| Prove theorems about lines and angles. Theorems include the following: Vertical angles are congruent; when a transversal crosses parallel lines, alternate interior angles are congruent and corresponding angles are congruent; and points on a perpendicular bisector of a line segment are exactly those equidistant from the segment's endpoints. *CCSS.Math.Content.HSG-CO.C.9* Prove theorems about triangles. Theorems include the following: Measures of interior angles of a triangle sum to 180°, base angles of isosceles triangles are congruent, the segment joining midpoints of two sides of a triangle is parallel to the third side and half the length, and the medians of a triangle meet at a point. *CCSS.Math.Content.HSG-CO.C.10* | When solving problems involving relationships between interior and exterior angles of a triangle, can students use characteristics and properties to compare angle measures? | Properties of Angles (p. 135) |

*(Continued)*

(Continued)

| Common Core Mathematical Content | Related Question | Probe Name |
|---|---|---|
| Prove theorems about parallelograms. Theorems include the following: Opposite sides are congruent, opposite angles are congruent, the diagonals of a parallelogram bisect each other, and, conversely, rectangles are parallelograms with congruent diagonals.<br><br>CCSS.Math.Content.HSG-CO.C.11 | Can students use properties of parallelograms to prove whether a figure is a parallelogram? | Is It a Parallelogram? (p. 141) |
| Identify the shapes of two-dimensional cross sections of three-dimensional objects, and identify three-dimensional objects generated by rotations of two-dimensional objects.<br><br>CCSS.Math.Content.HSG-GMD.B.4 | When working with three-dimensional figures, can students use characteristics to identify shapes? | Names of the Shape (p. 147) |
| Identify and describe relationships among inscribed angles, radii, and chords. Include the relationship between central, inscribed, and circumscribed angles; inscribed angles on a diameter are right angles; and the radius of a circle is perpendicular to the tangent where the radius intersects the circle.<br><br>CCSS.Math.Content.HSG-C.A.2 | When solving problems with circles, can students identify and use relationships among central and inscribed angles to solve measurement problems? | Circles and Angles (p. 152)<br><br>Variation: Inscribed Angles (p. 157)<br><br>Variation: Circle Theorems (p. 158) |
| Use trigonometric ratios and the Pythagorean theorem to solve right triangles in applied problems.<br><br>CCSS.Math.Content.HSG-SRT.C.8 | When solving for unknown side lengths or angle measures in right triangles, can students recognize correct trigonometric ratios to use? | Trigonometric Ratios (p. 159)<br><br>Variation: Laws of Sine and Cosine (p. 164) |
| Use volume formulas for cylinders, pyramids, cones, and spheres to solve problems.<br><br>CCSS.Math.Content.HSG-GMD.A.3<br><br>Use trigonometric ratios and the Pythagorean theorem to solve right triangles in applied problems.<br><br>CCSS.Math.Content.HSG-SRT.C.8 | Do students recognize what various geometric formulas are used for? | Geometry Formulas Card Sort (p. 165) |

Take a look at the variations that are available with some of the Probes in this chapter. All of these variations address geometry ideas but may extend the idea or offer a different structure for administering them. When available, variation Probes follow the Teacher Notes and associated reproducibles for the related original Probe.

**Properties of Angles**

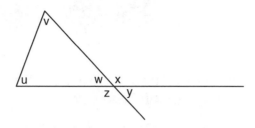

Use the above figure to determine if the statement is true or false.

| Circle the correct answer. | Explain your choice. |
| --- | --- |
| **1.**<br><br>*m∠w < m∠y*<br><br>a. True<br><br>b. False<br><br>c. Not enough information | |
| **2.**<br><br>*m∠x + m∠y = 180°*<br><br>a. True<br><br>b. False<br><br>c. Not enough information | |
| **3.**<br><br>*m∠u + m∠v = m∠x*<br><br>a. True<br><br>b. False<br><br>c. Not enough information | |
| **4.**<br><br>*m∠x + m∠u > 180°*<br><br>a. True<br><br>b. False<br><br>c. Not enough information | |

## Teacher Notes: Properties of Angles

### Questions to Consider About the Key Mathematical Concepts

When solving problems involving relationships between interior and exterior angles of a triangle, can students use characteristics and properties to compare angle measures? To what extent do they

- make sense of the relationships between interior and exterior angles of a triangle and use the properties of triangles and angles to compare angle measures?
- use geometric reasoning to compare measures of angles given statements about a figure?
- describe how characteristics and properties of angles and triangles are used to reason about the truth of a given statement?

### Common Core Connection (CCSS.Math.Content.HSG-CO.C.9)

**Grade:** High School

**Domain:** Geometry

**Cluster:**

**Prove geometric theorems.**

C9. Prove theorems about lines and angles. Theorems include the following: Vertical angles are congruent; when a transversal crosses parallel lines, alternate interior angles are congruent and corresponding angles are congruent; and points on a perpendicular bisector of a line segment are exactly those equidistant from the segment's endpoints.

### Common Core Connection (CCSS.Math.Content.HSG-CO.C.10)

**Grade:** High School

**Domain:** Geometry

**Cluster:**

**Prove geometric theorems.**

C10. Prove theorems about triangles. Theorems include the following: Measures of interior angles of a triangle sum to 180°, base angles of isosceles triangles are congruent, the segment joining midpoints of two sides of a triangle is parallel to the third side and half the length, and the medians of a triangle meet at a point.

## *U*ncovering Student Understanding About the Key Concepts

Using the Properties of Angles Probe can provide the following information about how the students are thinking about angle relationships.

*Do they*

- recognize congruent and supplementary relationships of angles based on properties?

OR

- use logical reasoning to analyze angle relationships?

OR

*Do they*

- use intuitive rules to incorrectly assume congruency?

- use inappropriate mental images about angles of a triangle?

## *E*xploring Excerpts From Educational Resources and Related Research

Areas of consideration:

The complexity of defining and measuring angles, given students' prior experiences with measurement, combine to make the concept of angle another challenging idea in geometry. [Students sometimes define angles] by referring to the elements involved in an angle such as line segments, rays, an intersection point, and/or the area between the rays (Keiser, Klee, and Fitch 2003). When students measure angles, once again, many do not think in terms of rotation. They search for a way to apply their previous knowledge of static measurement to situations of angle measure (Clements 2003). Some students who attempt to apply static measures to angle decide angle measure is determined by the distance between the two rays and/or segments of the angle. Other students decide angle measure is determined by the area between the rays and/or segments. (Driscoll, DiMatteo, Nikula, & Egan, 2007, p. 83)

Although students can logically organize ideas at van Hieles Level 3, "they still do not grasp that logical deduction is the method for establishing geometric truths." (National Council of Teachers of Mathematics [NCTM], 2003, p. 153)

Students refer to geometric properties and motions in their justifications, although they are not always accurate. Much remains for students to learn about congruence. (NCTM, 2003, p. 161)

When people think they do not always use definitions of concepts, but rather, concept images—a combination of all the mental pictures and properties that have been associated with the concept

(Vinner & Hershkowitz, 1980). Students who not only know a correct verbal description of a concept but also have strongly associated a specific visual image, or concept image, with the concept may have difficulty applying the verbal description correctly. (NCTM, 2003, p. 163)

## Surveying the Prompts and Selected Responses in the Probe

The Probe consists of four selected response items, each related to a common figure. The prompts and selected responses are designed to elicit understandings and common difficulties as described below:

| *If a student chooses* | *It is likely that the student* |
|---|---|
| 1. b, 2. a, 3. a, and 4. c<br><br>(correct responses) | • reasons correctly about the relationships of angles in a triangle. The student likely has an understanding of linear pairs, vertical angles, sum of interior angles, and properties of exterior angles. [See Sample Student Responses 1, 2, and 3]<br><br>*Look for indication of the student's understanding in the written explanations of how the student got the answer.* |
| 1. a, 4. a or 4. b | • uses intuitive rules based on what the angle measures look like. The student's answer is likely based on a perception of the measures instead of what is actually known. Some students reason that because the angles in Question 4 are connected by a line they must be supplementary (add to 180°). [See Sample Student Responses 4, 5, and 6] |
| 1. c, 2. b, 2. c, 3. b, and 3. c | • does not recognize the linear pair in Question 2 or reasons the angles might not be supplementary (add to 180°) because there are no measures given to prove it. The student also might not understand the property of an exterior angle measure being equal to the sum of its remote interior angles (Question 3). [See Sample Student Responses 4, 5, and 6] |

## Teaching Implications and Considerations

Ideas for eliciting more information from students about their understanding and difficulties:

- What different types of angles can be seen in the figure?
- What are vertical angles? Do you see any in the figure? What do you know about their measures?
- What is a linear pair? Do you see any in the figure? What do you know about them?

- What is an exterior angle? Do you see any in the figure?
- What do you know about the measure of an exterior angle based on the angle adjacent to it? What do you know about an exterior angle based on other interior angles beside the one adjacent to it (remote interior angles)?
- Which properties of triangles are about angles?
- Can you use any of the properties about triangles to compare the angles?
- What is the sum of the interior angles of a triangle?
- If you extended the rays in the figure, would it change any of the angle measures? If the student states yes to this question, have him or her actually measure the angles, extend the rays, and then measure the angles again.

Ideas for planning instruction in response to what you learned from the results of administering the Probe:

- Use a variety of mental imagery and kinesthetic opportunities to build understanding of geometric concepts.
- Give students opportunities to discover geometric properties instead of telling them or having them read about them.
- Provide practice with multiple examples of varying angle orientations and ray lengths to allow students different visual experiences.
- Allow students to progress through van Hiele's first three levels of geometric thinking. The levels are Level 1: Visual, Level 2: Descriptive/ Analytic, and Level 3: Abstract/Relational.
- Include practice and discussion of logical reasoning and justification as part of students' daily geometric learning.

## Sample Student Responses to Properties of Angles

### Responses That Suggest Understanding

*Sample Student Response 1*

Probe Item 1: Student chose b (False). Angles *w* and *y* are vertical angles, so they are congruent.

Probe Item 2: Student chose a (True). Angles *x* and *y* are a linear pair (supplementary), so the sum of their measures equals 180°.

Probe Item 3: Student chose a (True). The sum of the measures of two remote interior angles of a triangle equals the measure of the exterior angle of the third angle.

Probe Item 4: Student chose c (Not enough information). Because the angle measures could be anything, we do not know for sure if *x* and *u* are greater than 180°. Angle *u* could be 30°, and *x* could be 115°.

*(Continued)*

(Continued)

*Sample Student Response 2*

Probe Item 1: Student chose b (False). The angles are across from each other, so are the same measure.

Probe Item 2: Student chose a (True). The angles form a line, and a line is equal to 180°.

*Sample Student Response 3*

Probe Item 4: Student chose c (Not enough information). We are not allowed to assume things in geometry!

**Responses That Suggest Difficulty**

*Sample Student Response 4*

Probe Item 1: Student chose a (True). Angle *w* looks smaller than angle *y*, so I am thinking this statement is true.

Probe Item 3: Student chose c (Not enough information). We would be guessing if we answered true or false as we have no idea what the angle measurements are.

*Sample Student Response 5*

Probe Item 3: Student chose b (False). Angle *x* looks a lot bigger than the other two put together.

Probe Item 4: Student chose a (True). Angle *u* looks greater than *w* and *w* + *x* = 180° so *u* + *x* would have to be greater than 180°.

*Sample Student Response 6*

Probe Item 1: Student chose c (Not enough information). As we are not given any information about the angles, we do not know if one is larger than the other.

Probe Item 4: Student chose b (False). *x* and *u* are on the same line, so they equal 180°.

## Is It a Parallelogram?

| Circle Yes or No. | Explain your choice. |
|---|---|
| A.<br><br>Yes　　　No | |
| B.<br><br>Yes　　　No | |
| C.<br><br>Yes　　　No | |
| D.<br><br>Yes　　　No | |
| E.<br><br>Yes　　　No | |
| F.<br> 75° 75°<br>Yes　　　No | |
| G.<br><br>Yes　　　No | |

## Teacher Notes: Is It a Parallelogram?

### Questions to Consider About the Key Mathematical Concepts

Can students use properties of parallelograms to prove whether a figure is a parallelogram? To what extent do they

- make sense of information given and needed to represent a parallelogram?
- reason about whether enough or appropriate information is given for proving a figure is a parallelogram?
- describe the different ways to prove a figure is a parallelogram?

### Common Core Connection (CCSS.Math.Content.HSG-CO.C.11)

**Grade:** High School

**Domain:** Geometry

**Cluster:**

**Prove geometric theorems.**

C11. Prove theorems about parallelograms. Theorems include the following: Opposite sides are congruent, opposite angles are congruent, the diagonals of a parallelogram bisect each other, and, conversely, rectangles are parallelograms with congruent diagonals.

### Uncovering Student Understanding About the Key Concepts

Using the Is It a Parallelogram? Probe can provide the following information about how the students are thinking about properties of parallelograms.

| *Do they* | | *Do they* |
|---|---|---|
| • know that a parallelogram is a quadrilateral? | OR | • overgeneralize that any figures with parallel lines can be parallelograms? |
| • use the information given without assuming additional information? | OR | • assume certain properties based on looks, not fact? |

## Exploring Excerpts From Educational Resources and Related Research

Areas of consideration:

There are many different ways of classifying geometric shapes. Students have difficulty identifying and describing the defining properties of a classification. (Stepans et al., 2005, p. 233)

A construct that has been applied extensively to geometric thinking and learning is that of the concept image—a combination of all the mental pictures and properties that have been associated with the concept (Vinner & Hershkowitz, 1980). Students often use concept images rather than the definitions of concepts in their reasoning. (NCTM, 2003, p. 155)

The construct of concept images suggests that although diagrams and pictures can support geometric reasoning, they bring their own set of problems. Students often attribute characteristics of a drawing to the geometric object it represents, fail to understand that drawings do not necessarily represent all known information about the object represented, and attempt to draw figures so that they preserve both viewing perspective and the students' knowledge about the properties of the object being drawn (Parzysz, 1988). Instructional attention to diagrams, such as using multiple drawings for a proof problem and discussing diagrams explicitly, may be helpful. (NCTM, 2003, p. 155)

## Surveying the Prompts and Selected Responses in the Probe

The Probe consists of seven separate selected response items. The prompts and selected responses are designed to elicit understandings and common difficulties as described below:

| If a student chooses | It is likely that the student |
|---|---|
| D. and F. Yes, No for all other choices (correct responses) | • has an understanding of different ways to prove figures are parallelograms and does not assume any information not actually given. A quadrilateral can be proven to be a parallelogram if one or more of the following is true: (1) both pairs of opposite sides are parallel, (2) both pairs of opposite sides are congruent (Figure D), (3) both pairs of opposite angles are congruent (Figure F), (4) one pair of opposite sides is parallel and congruent, or |

*(Continued)*

(Continued)

| If a student chooses | It is likely that the student |
|---|---|
| | (5) diagonals bisect each other. [See Sample Student Response 1]<br><br>*Look for indication of the student's understanding in the written explanations of how the student got the answer.* |
| B. and/or E. Yes | • is assuming information about the angles that are not specifically labeled as right angles. Although two right angles are given in each figure, it cannot be assumed that the remaining two are also right angles (even though they appear to be so). The figures drawn below are with the same markings but with angles that do not appear to be 90°. [See Sample Student Response 2]<br><br>B.    E. |
| C. Yes | • does not understand the basic properties of a parallelogram. A parallelogram is a quadrilateral (a four-sided polygon). Often students will overgeneralize that if opposite sides of a figure are parallel, then the figure must be a parallelogram as in Figure C, even though there are more than four sides. [See Sample Student Response 3] |
| A. and/or G. Yes | • notices some properties of parallelograms in each figure and assumes one or both of the figures represent a parallelogram. In Figure A, students often see the markings for parallel lines and automatically assume the figure is a parallelogram. In Figure G, two pairs of sides look congruent but (1) they are not labeled as congruent and (2) they are not opposite each other. One pair of opposite angles is congruent, but no information is given about the other pair. [See Sample Student Responses 2 and 3] |

## Teaching Implications and Considerations

Ideas for eliciting more information from students about their understanding and difficulties:

• What are the properties of a parallelogram? (It is a quadrilateral with opposite sides parallel, opposites sides congruent, opposite angles congruent, consecutive angles supplementary, and diagonals bisecting each other.)

- What things do you need to know about a figure to prove it is a parallelogram? Is there more than one way to prove a figure is a parallelogram?
- What specific information are you given about this figure?
- What do "tick" marks and "arc" marks represent? What marks represent congruency in angles? In segments? What marks represent parallel lines?
- If angles and lines are not marked as congruent, can you assume they are congruent? If angles are not marked as right angles, can you assume they are right angles?
- If there is not enough information, what else would you need to know to prove the figure is a parallelogram?

Ideas for planning instruction in response to what you learned from the results of administering the Probe:

- Have students explore parallelograms (with technology or paper, rulers, and protractors) to discover the properties of parallelograms. This gives them ownership of the information.
- When drawing parallelograms (or any figures), completely label the figure with pertinent information (symbols) so students do not think they can assume information that is not actually given. Accurately label and represent right angles, angle or segment congruency, and parallel lines.
- Give various examples of figures that look like parallelograms but not enough information is given for proof. These types of problems allow for great discussions to solidify the concept.
- Draw figures of parallelograms but leave out some information that is needed to prove it. Ask students, "What other piece(s) of information is needed for proof?" Different students might come up with different pieces of information, which can lead to great classroom discussions.

### Sample Student Responses to Is It a Parallelogram?

**Responses That Suggest Understanding**

*Sample Student Response 1*

Probe Item A: Student chose No. There is not enough information given as we only know that one pair of opposite sides is parallel. Plus it doesn't even look like a parallelogram!

Probe Item B: Student chose No. It looks like a rectangle, which is a parallelogram, but the two bottom angles could be something other than 90°.

Probe Item C: Student chose No. This isn't even a quadrilateral!

*(Continued)*

(Continued)

Probe Item D: Student chose Yes. Two pairs of opposite side are congruent, so it is a parallelogram.

Probe Item E: Student chose No. This looks like a square, but I don't think there is enough information to tell what the other two angles actually are, so I am going with no.

Probe Item F: Student chose Yes. This one shows the opposite angles being the same, so it is a parallelogram.

Probe Item G: Student chose No. Doesn't even look like one plus there isn't enough info to prove anything.

**Responses That Suggest Difficulty**

*Sample Student Response 2*

Probe Item A: Student chose Yes. Opposite sides are parallel.

Probe Item B: Student chose Yes. All the angles are 90°, so this is a rectangle, which is a type of parallelogram.

Probe Item E: Student chose Yes. All of the angles are 90°, so this one is a square.

*Sample Student Response 3*

Probe Item C: Student chose Yes. The opposite sides are all parallel.

Probe Item G: Student chose Yes. Two sets of sides are the same and one set of angles, so this would be a parallelogram.

**Names of the Shape**

| Circle all correct names for each shape. | Explain your thinking. |
|---|---|
| **1.** <br><br>Polyhedron<br>Polygon<br>Triangular prism<br>Triangular pyramid<br>Pentagonal pyramid | |
| **2.** <br><br>Polyhedron<br>Polygon<br>Triangular prism<br>Triangular pyramid<br>Rectangular prism | |
| **3.** <br><br>Polyhedron<br>Polygon<br>Triangular prism<br>Triangular pyramid<br>Cone | |

## Teacher Notes: Names of the Shape

### **Q**uestions to Consider About the Key Mathematical Concepts

When working with three-dimensional figures, can students use characteristics to identify shapes? To what extent do they

- make sense of a two-dimensional drawing representing a three-dimensional figure?
- describe characteristics (or key features) of the figures that can be used to identify them?

---

**Common Core Connection
(CCSS.Math.Content.HSG-GMD.B.4)**

**Grade:** High School

**Domain:** Geometry

**Cluster:**

**Visualize relationships between two-dimensional and three-dimensional objects.**

B4. Identify the shapes of two-dimensional cross sections of three-dimensional objects, and identify three-dimensional objects generated by rotations of two-dimensional objects.

---

### **U**ncovering Student Understanding About the Key Concepts

Using the Names of the Shape Probe can provide the following information about how the students are thinking about three-dimensional figures.

*Do they*

- understand that polyhedra are three-dimensional figures (solids) with polygons for all faces?

OR

- recognize the difference between pyramids and prisms?

OR

*Do they*

- see all three-dimensional figures as polyhedra, including ones with nonpolygon faces?

- interchange the labels *pyramid* and *prism* (especially when a triangular prism is not sitting on its base)?

*Do they*

- identify pyramids and prisms by the shape of their base?

OR

*Do they*

- identify polyhedra by whatever side the figure is "sitting" on?

## Exploring Excerpts From Educational Resources and Related Research

Areas of consideration:

Many students [are] focused on shallow knowledge and skills, not analysis using special reasoning and critical thinking. Students were more comfortable with flat surfaces that they could see on activity sheets or draw on their papers. It was not as easy for them to represent a three-dimensional surface on a two-dimensional plane. (Circello & Filkins, 2012, p. 341)

There are many different ways of classifying geometric shapes. Students have difficulty identifying and describing the defining properties of a classification. (Stepans et al., 2005, p. 233)

## Surveying the Prompts and Selected Responses in the Probe

The Probe consists of three selected response items. The prompts and selected responses are designed to elicit understandings and common difficulties as described below:

| *If a student chooses* | *It is likely that the student* |
|---|---|
| 1. Polyhedron and pentagonal pyramid<br><br>2. Polyhedron and triangular prism<br><br>3. Cone<br><br>(correct responses) | • understands that polyhedra are solids (three-dimensional figures) with polygon-shaped sides (faces). Prisms have two bases that are parallel, congruent polygons. Pyramids have one polygonal base and three or more triangular faces (lateral) that meet at a point called the apex. Prisms and pyramids are named by the shape of their bases. A cone (Figure 3) is not a polyhedron as its sides are not made up of polygons. [See Sample Student Response 1]<br><br>*Look for indication of the student's understanding in the written explanations of how the student got the answer.* |

*(Continued)*

(Continued)

| If a student chooses | It is likely that the student |
|---|---|
| Any other response | • considers most solids to be polyhedra or, in a few cases, none of them to be as the student likely does not know the meaning of word *polyhedron*. Many students confuse Figure 2 with a pyramid when the solid is not sitting on its base (as shown in the probe). Students incorrectly consider the top edge to be the apex. Many students also have difficulty seeing three-dimensional figures drawn two-dimensionally and cannot process the attributes shown in the drawing. [See Sample Student Responses 2, 3, and 4] |

## Teaching Implications and Considerations

Ideas for eliciting more information from students about their understanding and difficulties:

- Does the shape of the solid change if it is "sitting" on a different face?
- What is the shape of the figure's base? Does the base change if we move the figure around?
- What are the shapes of the other faces?
- Are all of the faces polygons? What is a polygon?
- How many bases are there in the figure? If two, what type of polyhedron is it?
- If there is only one base, are the other faces triangles? Do they meet at a point (apex)? If so, what type of a polyhedron is it?
- What face(s) do we use to name a polyhedron?
- If not all of the sides are polygons, is it considered a polyhedron? What are some non-polyhedra solids that we see in everyday living? What are their geometric names?

Ideas for planning instruction in response to what you learned from the results of administering the Probe:

- Take some time at the beginning of a three-dimensional unit to create models of polyhedra and non-polyhedra from prepared nets or allow students to create their own. This allows students to transfer the two-dimensional shape into a three-dimensional one physically and cognitively.
- Allow students to use three-dimensional models (preferably ones they create) when solving three-dimensional problems.
- Sometimes you can create two-dimensional representations from the shadows of three-dimensional solids. Have your students try it!

- Have students connect various three-dimensional figures with actual objects they see on a daily basis.
- Have in-depth discussions on what side (for pyramids) and sides (for prisms) are the base(s).
- Have students compare and contrast prisms and pyramids and also polyhedron and non-polyhedron shapes.

## Sample Student Responses to Names of the Shape

### Responses That Suggest Understanding

*Sample Student Response 1*

Probe Item 1: Student chose polyhedron and pentagonal pyramid. As it is a three-dimensional figure with all sides made up of polygons, it is a polyhedron. The base is a five-sided polygon (pentagon) and all of the other sides meet at a point called the apex, so this is a pentagonal pyramid.

Probe Item 2: Student chose polyhedron and triangular prism. Same as number 1 for the polyhedron. This figure is not sitting on its base. The base is one of the triangular shaped sides. As there are two bases (parallel to each other), it is a prism.

Probe Item 3: Student chose cone. Not all the sides are polygons, so it is not a polyhedron. It is a cone.

### Responses That Suggest Difficulty

*Sample Student Response 2*

Probe Item 1: Student chose everything except triangular prism. This figure is made up of polygons that are put together, so it is a polygon and a polyhedron. It is a pyramid as it looks like one and there are triangles and a pentagon in it.

*Sample Student Response 3*

Probe Item 2: Student chose polyhedron and triangular pyramid. It is a polyhedron because all the sides are flat. It is a pyramid because it angles up to a point.

*Sample Student Response 4*

Probe Item 3: Student chose polyhedron, triangular pyramid, and cone. It is a three-dimensional object, so it is a polyhedron, and it meets at a point, so it is a pyramid. Its well-known name is a cone.

**Circles and Angles**

**1. A circle is drawn with center _O_ and the measure of angle _AOB_ is 75°.**

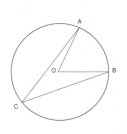

Three students were discussing whether angle _ACB_ could be found:

Student A. The measure of angle _ACB_ is 75°.

Student B. The measure of angle _ACB_ is 37.5°.

Student C. There is not enough information to find angle _ACB_.

Who do you agree with and why?

**2. A circle is drawn with a diameter _AB_, which has a length of 70 cm.**

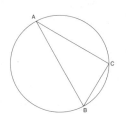

Three students were discussing whether angle _ACB_ could be found:

Student A. The measure of angle _ACB_ is 70°.

Student B. The measure of angle _ACB_ is 90°.

Student C. There is not enough information to find angle _ACB_.

Who do you agree with and why?

## Teacher Notes: Circles and Angles

### Questions to Consider About the Key Mathematical Concepts

When solving problems with circles, can students identify and use relationships among central and inscribed angles to solve measurement problems? To what extent do they

- make sense of circular drawings that include angle and arc measures?
- reason about the relationships between and among angles drawn in a circle and intercepted arcs?
- describe the relationships between central and inscribed angles and their intercepted arcs?

### Common Core Connection (CCSS.Math.Content.HSG-C.A.2)

**Grade:** High School

**Domain:** Geometry

**Cluster:**

**Understand and apply theorems about circles.**

A2. Identify and describe relationships among inscribed angles, radii, and chords. Include the relationship between central, inscribed, and circumscribed angles; inscribed angles on a diameter are right angles; and the radius of a circle is perpendicular to the tangent where the radius intersects the circle.

### Uncovering Student Understanding About the Key Concepts

Using the Circles and Angles Probe can provide the following information about how the students are thinking about the relationships between angle and arc measures.

*Do they*

- recognize central and inscribed angles?   OR

- recognize and describe relationships between the measures of angles and their intercepted arc?   OR

- apply theorems about circles to find measures?   OR

*Do they*

- see lines drawn in a circle that happen to make angles?

- see the angles having nothing in common with each other or with their intercepted arc measure?

- try to guess measures based on the visual appearance of the angles or the lengths of the segments forming the angles?

## Exploring Excerpts From Educational Resources and Related Research

Areas of consideration:

Students may consider the linear distance between two rays such that the length of an angle's size depends on the length of the rays or the points along the rays used to perform the measurement. Often, students believe that the farther they travel out on the rays, the larger the angle gets. This also leads to difficulty in understanding the effects scaling has on angle. Some students believe that if a right angle is scaled up so that the segments of the angle are now twice as long as the original, the angle has increased as well (Keiser 2004). Finally, some students think of angle measure in terms of area between segments. (Driscoll et al., 2007, p. 84)

Students often use concept images rather than definitions of concepts in their reasoning. These concept images are adversely affected by inappropriate instruction. For example, the concept image of an obtuse angle as requiring a horizontal ray might result from the limited set of examples students see in textbooks. (NCTM, 2003, p. 155)

## Surveying the Prompts and Selected Responses in the Probe

The Probe consists of two "math talk" items. The prompts and selected responses are designed to elicit understandings and common difficulties as described below:

| If a student chooses | It is likely that the student |
|---|---|
| 1. Student B, 2. Student B<br><br>(correct responses) | • recognizes and can use the relationships between central angles, intercepted arc measures, and inscribed angles. For Question 1, the central angle ($\angle AOB$) and the inscribed angle ($\angle ACB$) share an intercepted arc (arc $AB$); therefore, the measure of the central angle is the same as the arc measure, and the measure of the inscribed angle is $\frac{1}{2}$ the arc measure. For Question 2, the intercepted arc for the inscribed angle ($\angle ACB$) is the diameter ($AB$), which has a measure of 180°. This allows the measure of the intercepted arc to be found by taking $\frac{1}{2}$ of 180°. [See Sample Student Responses 1 and 2]<br><br>*Look for indication of the student's understanding in the written explanations of how the student got the answer.* |

| If a student chooses | It is likely that the student |
|---|---|
| 1. Student A,<br>1. Student C,<br>2. Student A,<br>2. Student C | • does not understand the relationships between central angles and their intercepted arc measures (the measures are the same) or between inscribed angles and their intercepted arc measures (the measure of the angle is $\frac{1}{2}$ the measure of the intercepted arc). [See Sample Student Responses 3, 4, and 5] |

## Teaching Implications and Considerations

Ideas for eliciting more information from students about their understanding and difficulties:

- What type of angle is ∠AOB? What is the intercepted arc for ∠AOB?
- What is an arc?
- What is the relationship between a central angle and its intercepted arc?
- What type of angle is ∠ACB? What is the intercepted arc for ∠ACB?
- What is the relationship between an inscribed angle and its intercepted arc?
- What does it mean for an angle to be inscribed on a diameter? What does it tell us about the angle?
- If a central angle and an inscribed angle share the same intercepted arc, what does it tell us about their measures?

Ideas for planning instruction in response to what you learned from the results of administering the Probe:

- Allow students time to explore the measures of angles with a protractor (or cutting paper and comparing) until they realize there are relationships between and among central and inscribed angles that have the same intercepted arc.
- Give students opportunities to "see" and explore different types of angles drawn in various places on a circle. Make sure examples are not always drawn in the same way or place in the circle. "Pictures need to be varied so that students are not led to form incorrect concept images" (NCTM, 2003, p. 156).
- Use of technology to explore geometric concepts can be fun, creative, and allow students to construct ideas and discover relationships.

# Sample Student Responses to Circles and Angles

## Responses That Suggest Understanding

### Sample Student Response 1

Probe Item 1: Student chose Student B. Student B is correct because *AOD* is a central angle, and its measure is the same as its intercepting arc (*AB*). This means arc *AB* is 75°. Once you know this, you can figure out *ACB* because it is an inscribed angle, which has a measure of $\frac{1}{2}$ of its intercepting arc, which is also arc *AB*.

### Sample Student Response 2

Probe Item 2: Student chose Student B. This was a tricky one as there was some information given that was not needed. The length of the diameter *AB* is not needed. You only need to know that it is a diameter and has a measure of 180° to solve this problem. Angle *ACB* is inscribed with the diameter as its intercepting arc, so it measures $\frac{1}{2}$ of 180°, which of course is 90°.

## Responses That Suggest Difficulty

### Sample Student Response 3

Probe Item 1: Student chose Student A. I remember rules that state that angles are equal to the arcs they are attached to.

Probe Item 2: Student chose Student A. Same as Question 1; angles are equal to the arc measure.

### Sample Student Response 4

Probe Item 1: Student chose Student C. The two angles are not related, so we would need to have more information to solve this problem.

### Sample Student Response 5

Probe Item 2: Student chose Student C. Triangle *ABC* looks like a right triangle, which would make angle *ACB* 90°, but I think we need more information to actually prove it.

## Variation: Inscribed Angles

A circle is drawn with a diameter *AB,* which measures 70 cm. Students were discussing whether angle *ACB* could be found. Who do you agree with and why?

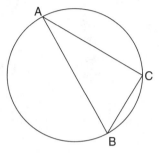

The measure of angle ACB is 70°.

Jack

The measure of angle *ACB* is 90°.

Xavier

There is not enough information to find angle *ACB*.

Michelle

Who do you agree with and why?

## Variation: Circle Theorems

5.4Vb

Choose if each statement is true or false and justify your choice.

| Circle the correct answer. | Justify your choice. |
|---|---|
| 1. The measure of an inscribed angle is equal to its intercepted arc measure.<br><br>a. True<br><br>b. False | |
| 2. An inscribed angle whose rays intersect the endpoints of a diameter of a circle is always a right angle.<br>a. True<br><br>b. False | |
| 3. An inscribed angle's measure is always double that of a central angle that shares the same intercepting arc.<br>a. True<br><br>b. False | |
| 4. Inscribed angles with a common intercepting arc are supplementary.<br><br>a. True<br><br>b. False | |
| 5. Opposite angles in an inscribed quadrilateral add up to 180°.<br><br>a. True<br><br>b. False | |

## Trigonometric Ratios

5.5

Decide whether each trigonometric ratio could be used to find the missing side or angle.

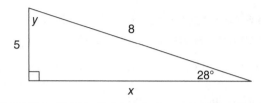

| **1. To find *x*:** | Circle one: | Explain your choices: |
|---|---|---|
| a. $\sin 28 = \dfrac{x}{8}$ | Yes    No | |
| b. $\cos 28 = \dfrac{x}{8}$ | Yes    No | |
| c. $\tan 28 = \dfrac{x}{5}$ | Yes    No | |
| d. $\tan 28 = \dfrac{5}{x}$ | Yes    No | |

| **2. To find *y*:** | Circle one: | Explain your choices: |
|---|---|---|
| a. $y = \dfrac{\frac{5}{8}}{\sin}$ | Yes    No | |
| b. $y = \sin^{-1}\left(\dfrac{5}{8}\right)$ | Yes    No | |
| c. $y = \dfrac{\frac{5}{8}}{\cos}$ | Yes    No | |
| d. $y = \cos^{-1}\left(\dfrac{5}{8}\right)$ | Yes    No | |

# Teacher Notes:
# Trigonometric Ratios

## Questions to Consider About the Key Mathematical Concepts

When solving for unknown side lengths or angle measures in right triangles, can students recognize correct trigonometric ratios to use? To what extent do they

- make sense of which ratio(s) to use based on the hypotenuse and the adjacent and opposite sides of a right triangle?
- reason about whether to use sine, cosine, or tangent to find an unknown measure?
- describe how trigonometric ratios can be used to create a proportion to find an unknown side length or angle measure?

---

### Common Core Connection
### (CCSS.Math.Content.HSG-SRT.C.8)

**Grade:** High School

**Domain:** Geometry

**Cluster:**

**Define trigonometric ratios and solve problems involving right triangles.**

C8. Use trigonometric ratios and the Pythagorean theorem to solve right triangles in applied problems.

---

## Uncovering Student Understanding About the Key Concepts

Using the Trigonometric Ratios Probe can provide the following information about how the students are thinking about ratios with right triangles.

*Do they*

- know the correct ratios for sine, cosine, and tangent?

- determine which legs of the triangle are the opposite and the adjacent sides based on a particular angle?

OR

OR

*Do they*

- confuse which side lengths to use in the ratios?

- confuse the opposite and adjacent sides, or not realize they change based on which angle is being used as a reference angle?

*Do they*

- use inverse trigonometric functions to find angle measures (sin⁻¹, cos⁻¹, or tan⁻¹)?

OR

*Do they*

- not realize that inverse functions are needed to find missing angle measures, oftentimes "getting rid of" the word *sin, cos,* or *tan* by dividing both sides of the equation by it (using it as a variable)?

# Exploring Excerpts From Educational Resources and Related Research

Areas of consideration:

Trigonometry is an area of mathematics that students believe to be particularly difficult and abstract compared with the other subjects of mathematics. Three generalizations were made because of their relationship to Piaget's description of formal operations that could be drawn from the study on misconceptions. These three generalizations are

1. Many misconceptions are related to a concept that produces a mathematical object and symbol. For example, sine is a concept and symbol of trigonometric functions.
2. Many misconceptions are related to process: the ability to use operations, for example, as representing the result of calculation of sin 300° and value of sin 300°.
3. Many misconceptions are related to procept that is, the ability to think of mathematical operations and object. Procept covers both concept and process. For example: sin $x$ is both a function and a value. In addition to this, Gray and Tall (1994) asserted that "procedural thinking," that is, the ability to think of mathematical operations and object as procept, is critical to the successful learning of mathematics. (Gur, 2009, p. 68)

# Surveying the Prompts and Selected Responses in the Probe

The Probe consists of two selected response items, each related to a common figure. The prompts and selected responses are designed to elicit understandings and common difficulties as described in the following table.

| If a student chooses | It is likely that the student |
|---|---|
| 1. a. No, b. Yes, c. No, and d. Yes<br><br>2. a. No, b. No, c. No, and d. Yes<br><br>(correct response) | • knows and understands the trigonometric ratios and can set up equations to find unknown side lengths (Question 1) and angle measures (Question 2). In the case of Question 2, the student realizes that the inverse function needs to be used to find the unknown angle measure. [See Sample Student Responses 1 and 2]<br><br>*Look for indication of the student's understanding in the written explanations of how the student got the answer.* |
| All other responses | • has not learned the trigonometric ratios or confuses which side lengths to use based on what is given. Students often mix up the adjacent and opposite sides. In Question 2, students often do not understand how to find an angle measure or incorrectly apply the inverse function. Many students see the trigonometric functions (sin, cos, and tan) as variables and use division to "undo" them. [See Sample Student Responses 3 and 4] |

# Teaching Implications and Considerations

Ideas for eliciting more information from students about their understanding and difficulties:

- What do the words *hypotenuse*, *adjacent*, and *opposite* mean?
- Based on the angle that is 28°, which side is opposite it? What is the length of that side?
- Based on the angle that is 28°, which angle is adjacent to it? What is the length of that side?
- Based on the angle that is $y$, which side is opposite it? What is the length of that side?
- Based on the angle that is $y$, which angle is adjacent to it? What is the length of that side?
- How is finding an angle different from finding a side?
- What are the ratios for sine, cosine, and tangent? How are they similar? How are they different?
- What does sin $y$ (or cos $y$ or tan $y$) mean? Does it mean multiplication because they are right next to each other? (No)
- How do we "get rid of" the "sin" in the equation sin $x = \left(\dfrac{4}{5}\right)$?
- What does an inverse trigonometric function do? When do you use it?

Ideas for planning instruction in response to what you learned from the results of administering the Probe:

- Allow students many opportunities to explore right triangles thoroughly, with paper and pencil and with technology too.

- When drawing triangles, orient the triangles differently so students get a better understanding of opposite and adjacent sides. Use triangles that are labeled other than $\triangle ABC$.
- Have students ask themselves what each side is called (hypotenuse, adjacent, or opposite) in reference to a specific angle.
- SOH CAH TOA is a great way for students to remember the trigonometric ratios, especially if it is told via an exciting story of the land of the Trigs and chief SOH CAH TOA!
- As inverse trigonometric functions are probably new concepts for most students, provide various opportunities to explore "undoing" sin, cos, and tan with inverse functions. This will become second nature to them if they have many opportunities to use it and practice with it.

## Sample Student Responses to Trigonometric Ratios

### Responses That Suggest Understanding

*Sample Student Response 1*

Probe Item 1: Student chose No for a and c and Yes for b and d. I used SOH CAH TOA to decide which ones are correct. Based on the angle we are given (28°), the opposite side is "5," the adjacent side is "$x$," and of course the hypotenuse is "8." Using these and the rules (SOH CAH TOA), the only two that can be used is b and d. $\sin 28 = \frac{5}{8}$, which does not include $x$; $\tan 28 = \frac{5}{x}$, not $\frac{x}{5}$; and $\cos 28 = \frac{x}{8}$.

*Sample Student Response 2*

Probe Item 2: Student chose No for a, b, and c and Yes for d. As we are looking for $y$, we cannot have another unknown so cannot use the opposite side to angle $y$, which is $x$. This eliminates sin and tan. As we are looking for an unknown angle, we will need to use an inverse function, and choice d works! For choice c, we divide by cos instead of taking the inverse.

### Responses That Suggest Difficulty

*Sample Student Response 3*

Probe Item 1: Student chose Yes for a, b, c, and d. You can solve for $x$ in all of the equations.

Probe Item 2: Student chose Yes for a and c and No for b and d. To solve for $y$, you have to get it alone by dividing each side by what is next to it (sin or cos). Not sure what that −1 thing is.

*Sample Student Response 4*

Probe Item 1: Student chose No for c and d and Yes for a and b. c and d are not right because the adjacent side is 8, and there is no 8 in either equation.

## Variation: Laws of Sine and Cosine

Decide which law could be used to solve for the measures identified in the questions. The figure is not drawn to scale.

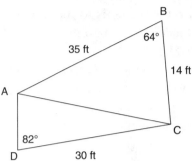

| **1. To find measure of *AC:*** | Explain your choice: |
|---|---|
| a. Law of cosines | |
| b. Law of sines | |
| c. Neither can be used | |
| **2. To find measure of angle *BCA:*** | Explain your choice: |
| a. Law of cosines | |
| b. Law of sines | |
| c. Neither can be used | |
| **3. To find the area of triangle *CAB:*** | Explain your choice: |
| a. Law of cosines | |
| b. Law of sines | |
| c. Neither can be used | |

5.6

# Geometry Formulas Card Sort

(Reproducible student cards follow Teacher Notes on p. 171.)

| | | | |
|---|---|---|---|
| **Area** | **Volume** | G. $\dfrac{x_2 + x_1}{2}, \dfrac{y_2 + y_1}{2}$ | H. $\dfrac{bh}{2}$ |
| **Distance** | **Other** | I. $\sqrt{(x_2 - x_1)^2 + (y_2 - y_1)^2}$ | J. $\dfrac{(b_1 + b_2)h}{2}$ |
| A. $Bh$ | B. $\dfrac{y_2 - y_1}{x_2 - x_1}$ | K. $2\pi r$ | L. $s^2$ |
| C. $\dfrac{4\pi r^3}{3}$ | D. $leg^2 + leg^2 = hyp^2$ | M. $\dfrac{Bh}{3}$ | N. $\pi r^2$ |
| E. $lw$ | F. $2l + 2w$ | | |

**Advance Preparation:** Create cards by photocopying and cutting. Separate the label cards (Area, Volume, Distance, Other) from the deck and shuffle the rest of the cards.

## Instructions:

1. Invite the student(s) to sort the cards into four piles: Area, Volume, Distance, and Other. Use the label cards to identify the piles.

2. As students finish the sort, give them the blank cards and ask them to create their own Area, Volume, Distance, and Other examples (one of each).

3. Either choose two cards for the student or ask the student to choose two cards from each pile. Ask the students to explain how they knew these cards should go in the pile.

## Teacher Notes:
## Geometry Formulas Card Sort

## **Q**uestions to Consider About the
## Key Mathematical Concepts

Do students recognize what various geometric formulas are used for? To what extent do they

- make sense of the myriad of formulas used in geometry?
- reason about the connections between and among various formulas?
- describe comparisons and/or differences among formulas when grouped together?

### Common Core Connection
### (CCSS.Math.Content.HSG-GMD.A.3)

**Grade:** High School

**Domain:** Geometry

**Cluster:**

**Explain volume formulas and use them to solve problems.**

A3. Use volume formulas for cylinders, pyramids, cones, and spheres to solve problems.

### Common Core Connection
### (CCSS.Math.Content.HSG-SRT.C.8)

**Grade:** High School

**Domain:** Geometry

**Cluster:**

**Define trigonometric ratios and solve problems involving right triangles.**

C8. Use trigonometric ratios and the Pythagorean theorem to solve right triangles in applied problems.

## **U**ncovering Student Understanding
## About the Key Concepts

Using the Geometry Formulas Card Sort Probe can provide the following information about how the students are thinking about connections among formulas.

| *Do they* | | *Do they* |
|---|---|---|
| • recognize individual formulas when placed with many others? | OR | • get confused and recognize few if any of the formulas? |
| • group formulas together by what they are used for? | OR | • group them together in the order in which they were learned (unit based)? |
| • justify the placement of the formulas in groups? | OR | • lack justification? |
| • have skills in regrouping various ways? | OR | • only see the formulas belonging to one group? |

# *E*xploring Excerpts From Educational Resources and Related Research

Areas of consideration:

Students often have preconceived ideas or even misconceptions and may know a list of steps or algorithms. Although they can perform these calculations, they may not always understand the concept or mathematical connections. (Hartweg, 2011, p. 41)

Arguably, the way mathematics problems are framed can make it challenging for algebraic and geometric reasoning to act in concert in a problem solver's brain. That is, if a problem asks for a numeric or quantitative outcome, it is often inviting and comfortable to think algebraically. Similarly, if the desired outcome has to do with shape, location, and so on of objects in space, than it is inviting and comfortable to think geometrically. In each case, the solver is likely to pay attention to different aspects of the problem. (Driscoll et al., 2007, p. 25)

Students do not associate the Theorem of Pythagoras with a statement about areas of squares. Rather they treat it as an algebraic statement about the lengths of sides of a right triangle. (Stepans et al., 2005, p. 234)

# *S*urveying the Prompts and Selected Responses in the Probe

The Probe consists of multiple examples of geometric formulas involving area, volume, distance, and other geometric concepts. The prompts and selected responses are designed to elicit understandings and common difficulties as described below:

| If a student chooses | It is likely that the student |
|---|---|
| Area: D, E, H, J, L, and N | • recognizes the basic area formulas. Some students will omit Card D (Pythagorean theorem) from this category as they do not see it as representing the areas of squares. Often this is because students are taught the theorem as a process and not allowed to explore its conceptual foundation. [See Sample Student Response 1]<br><br>*Look for indication of the student's understanding in the written explanations of how the student got the answer.* |
| Volume: A, C, and M | • recognizes the basic volume formulas. [See Sample Student Response 1] |
| Distance: D, F, I, and K | • recognizes perimeter as the distance around an object and circumference as the perimeter or distance around a circle. If the Pythagorean theorem is put in this group, the student most likely understands that the distance formula is derived from the Pythagorean theorem and that both formulas find a distance between two points. [See Sample Student Response 1] |
| Other: B and G | • knows what these two formulas are and sees them in a different category. Card B is the slope formula and Card G is the midpoint formula. [See Sample Student Response 1] |
| Any other choices | • either does not recognize the formulas or does not completely understand what can be found by using them. Many students do not recognize perimeter (especially circumference) and the Pythagorean theorem as finding distance. The capital letter B in the volume formulas sometimes confuses students as they think it is referring to a base instead of the area of a base. [See Sample Student Responses 2 and 3] |

## *T*eaching Implications and Considerations

Ideas for eliciting more information from students about their understanding and difficulties:

- What are some of the important formulas that we use in geometry (i.e., Pythagorean theorem, distance, midpoint, slope, perimeters, areas, volumes)?
- When you are finding areas (or perimeters or volumes) of various figures, what information do you need? What do these types of formulas have in common?

- Do we use some of these formulas in algebra? When or why?
- Do any of the formulas have similar looks, use similar letters, and so on?
- What does a capital B mean in the formulas? The lowercase b?
- Is area or volume squared? Which is cubed?
- How are formulas K and N similar? How are they different?
- The variables (sides of a triangle) in the Pythagorean theorem are squared. What does this mean?

Ideas for planning instruction in response to what you learned from the results of administering the Probe:

- When talking about perimeter, use the phrase "distance around an object" so students connect the two.
- When verbalizing "B," make sure everyone always states "the area of the base," not just "the base." This helps eliminate the confusion around equating formulas using B with area instead of volume.
- Do not use geometric formulas in isolation. Many of the formulas make for great explorations in algebra class and can be connected in many areas of mathematical learning. For complete understanding, students should see geometry in algebra and algebra in geometry.
- Do not assume that students have classification skills. Give them opportunities to practice these skills often and have discussions around them.
- Allow students to group and regroup the cards. This enables students to think outside the box and make connections that are not usually part of the regular curriculum. These connections allow student thinking to go higher on taxonomy scales.

### Sample Student Responses to Geometry Formulas Card Sort

**Responses That Suggest Understanding**

*Sample Student Response 1*

Probe Item Area: Student chose E, H, J, L, and N. $s^2$ is the area for a square, $lw$ is the area of a rectangle, $\frac{(b_1+b_2)h}{2}$ is the area of a trapezoid, $\pi r^2$ is the area of a circle, and $\frac{bh}{2}$ is the area of a triangle.

Probe Item Volume: Student chose A, C, and M. A big B means area of a base, so $Bh$ is the volume of a prism, $\frac{Bh}{3}$ is the volume of a pyramid, and $\frac{4\pi r^3}{3}$ is the volume of a sphere.

*(Continued)*

(Continued)

Probe Item Distance: Student chose D, F, I, and K. Perimeter is actually the distance around something, so we put the perimeter formulas in this one: $2l + 2w$ for rectangle and $2\pi r$ for circle (circumference). We also put in the distance formula (duh) and the Pythagorean theorem as it finds the length (distance) of a missing side of a right triangle.

Probe Item Other: Student chose B and G. We didn't see how slope and midpoint formulas could fit into the other three categories so we put them in their own.

**Responses That Suggest Difficulty**

*Sample Student Response 2*

Probe Item Volume: Student chose C. Volume is cubed, and C is the only one that has a cube in it.

*Sample Student Response 3*

Probe Item Distance: Student chose I. The only one that should be under this category is the distance formula (I).

Probe Item Other: Student chose B, D, E, F, and G. There are many that do not fit under area, volume, or distance. We put Cards B, D, E, F, and G in this section. B is slope, D is the Pythagorean theorem, E and F are perimeter formulas, and G we are not sure about.

**Geometry Formulas Cards**

5.6a

| | |
|---|---|
| **Area** | **Volume** |
| **Distance** | **Other** |
| A. <br><br> $Bh$ | B. <br><br> $\dfrac{y_2 - y_1}{x_2 - x_1}$ |
| C. <br><br> $\dfrac{4\pi r^3}{3}$ | D. <br><br> $leg^2 + leg^2 = hyp^2$ |
| E. <br><br> $lw$ | F. <br><br> $2l + 2w$ |

| | |
|---|---|
| G. $$\frac{x_2+x_1}{2}, \frac{y_2+y_1}{2}$$ | H. $$\frac{bh}{2}$$ |
| I. $$\sqrt{(x_2-x_1)^2+(y_2-y_1)^2}$$ | J. $$\frac{(b_1+b_2)h}{2}$$ |
| K. $$2\pi r$$ | L. $$s^2$$ |
| M. $$\frac{Bh}{3}$$ | N. $$2\pi r$$ |
| | |

# 6

# Statistics and Probability Probes

The content of the Probes in this chapter aligns with the standards for high school but is often taught in different courses across districts. The Probes and their variations are also relevant beyond the aligned course level for students in more advanced courses who have not yet met particular standards from previous courses as well as for students who have already met the standards in the current course.

We developed these Probes to address this critical area of focus for high school students, described in the standards (Council of Chief State School Officers [CCSSO], 2010) as follows:

- Represent data on two quantitative variables on a scatter plot and describe how the variables are related.
- Interpret the slope (rate of change) and the intercept (constant term) of a linear model in the context of the data.
- Represent data with plots on the real number line (dot plots, histograms, and box plots).
- Use statistics appropriate to the shape of the data distribution to compare center (median, mean) and spread (interquartile range, standard deviation) of two or more different data sets.
- Interpret differences in shape, center, and spread in the context of the data sets, accounting for possible effects of extreme data points (outliers).
- Understand that two events $A$ and $B$ are independent if the probability of $A$ and $B$ occurring together is the product of their probabilities, and use this characterization to determine if they are independent.

The content of the Probes in this chapter aligns with the standards for high school but is often taught in different courses across districts. The Probes and their variations are also relevant beyond the aligned course level for students in more advanced courses who have not yet met particular standards from previous courses as well as for students who have already met the standards in the current course.

- Apply the Addition Rule, $P(A \text{ or } B) = P(A) + P(B) - P(A \text{ and } B)$, and interpret the answer in terms of the model.
- Describe events as subsets of a sample space (the set of outcomes) using characteristics (or categories) of the outcomes, or as unions, intersections, or complements of other events (*or, and, not*).

The standards and their related questions, as well as the Probes associated with them, are shown in Table 6.1.

**Table 6.1**   Probability and Statistics Probes

| Common Core Mathematical Content | Related Question | Probe Name |
|---|---|---|
| Represent data on two quantitative variables on a scatter plot, and describe how the variables are related.<br><br>*CCSS.Math.Content.HHS-ID.B.6*<br><br>Interpret the slope (rate of change) and the intercept (constant term) of a linear model in the context of the data.<br><br>*CCSS.Math.Content.HHS-ID.C.7* | When analyzing linear data graphically, can students interpret the rate of change (slope) and *y*-intercept when the graph does not start at the origin? | Modeling With Linear Graphs (p. 176)<br><br>Variation: Scatter Plots (p. 181) |
| Represent data with plots on the real number line (dot plots, histograms, and box plots).<br><br>*CCSS.Math.Content.HSS-ID.A.1*<br><br>Use statistics appropriate to the shape of the data distribution to compare center (median, mean) and spread (interquartile range, standard deviation) of two or more different data sets.<br><br>*CCSS.Math.Content.HSS-ID.A.2*<br><br>Interpret differences in shape, center, and spread in the context of the data sets, accounting for possible effects of extreme data points (outliers).<br><br>*CCSS.Math.Content.HSS-ID.A.3* | When working with box plots, can students analyze and compare data sets without a given scale? | Comparing Data in Box Plots (p. 182)<br><br>Variation: Comparing Data in Box Plots (p. 189) |

| Common Core Mathematical Content | Related Question | Probe Name |
|---|---|---|
| Understand that two events $A$ and $B$ are independent if the probability of $A$ and $B$ occurring together is the product of their probabilities, and use this characterization to determine if they are independent.<br><br>CCSS.Math.Content.HSS-CP.A.2<br><br>Apply the Addition Rule, $P(A$ or $B) = P(A) + P(B) - P(A$ and $B)$, and interpret the answer in terms of the model.<br><br>CCSS.Math.Content.HSS-CP.B.7 | When working with probability problems, do students recognize when to apply addition or multiplication rules? | Probability (p. 190) |

Take a look at the variations that are available with some of the Probes in this chapter. All of these variations address statistics and probability ideas but may extend the idea or offer a different structure for administering them. When available, variation Probes follow the Teacher Notes and associated reproducibles for the related original Probe.

## Modeling With Linear Graphs

The following graph shows data that a group of students found on ice cream sales in dollars (*y* values) versus temperature in °C (*x* values). They drew a best-fit line and found the equation of the line to be $y = 19.5x + 100$. When the same data were entered into a graphing calculator and a regression model found, the equation was $y = 30x - 159.5$. Why is the best-fit equation so different from the regression model?

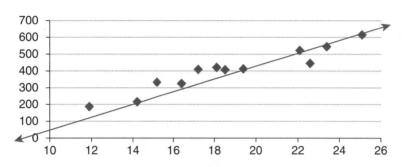

I think it is different because they did not find the best-fit line

McKayla

I think it is different because their graph does not show all of the *x* intervals.

Olivia

I think it is different because they probably didn't put the data into the calculator accurately.

Dylan

Who do you agree with and why?

# Teacher Notes: Modeling With Linear Graphs

## Questions to Consider About the Key Mathematical Concepts

When analyzing linear data graphically, can students interpret the rate of change (slope) and $y$-intercept when the graph does not start at the origin? To what extent do they

- make sense of graphs that do not have the horizontal and vertical axes meeting at the origin (inaccurate scales)?
- reason about the $y$-intercept when data are plotted on a graph not starting at the origin?
- describe the differences in equations based on data graphed accurately (graphing calculator) and data graphed inaccurately (by hand with scale errors)?

### Common Core Connection (CCSS.Math.Content.HHS-ID.B.6)

**Grade:** High School

**Domain:** Statistics and Probability

**Cluster:**

**Summarize, represent, and interpret data on two categorical and quantitative variables.**

B6. Represent data on two quantitative variables on a scatter plot, and describe how the variables are related.

6a Fit a function to the data; use functions fitted to data to solve problems in the context of the data. Use given functions or choose a function suggested by the context. Emphasize linear, quadratic, and exponential models.

6c Fit a linear function for a scatter plot that suggests a linear association.

### Common Core Connection (CCSS.Math.Content.HHS-ID.C.7)

**Grade:** High School

**Domain:** Statistics and Probability

**Cluster:**

**Interpret linear models.**

C7. Interpret the slope (rate of change) and the intercept (constant term) of a linear model in the context of the data.

# *U*ncovering Student Understanding About the Key Concepts

Using the Modeling With Linear Graphs Probe can provide the following information about how the students are thinking about key features of a graphical representation of a linear model.

*Do they*

- look at all features of the graph to find an accurate slope and *y*-intercept?

OR

- realize that changes in scale change the appearance of a graph?

OR

- realize that a change in scale and the way the graph looks might change the placement of a best-fit line?

*Do they*

- just look where the line of best fit crosses the *y*-axis and pick two points to find the slope of line drawn?

OR

- not realize scale as being a part of the graph to analyze and use for interpretation?

OR

- not attribute the placement of the best-fit line to be affected by the scale chosen?

# *E*xploring Excerpts From Educational Resources and Related Research

Areas of consideration:

Deciding on plot scales and on what data should be included in their plots poses a number of interesting challenges to students. Some students in Russell et al. (2002a) thought that plot scales should not extend beyond the range of observed values, whereas others argued that the scales should extend to include values that could have occurred or far enough at least to make a pleasant boundary. Without gaps along the scale representing nonoccurring [data], it is difficult to see clumping in the data or to judge the magnitude of the difference between various [data points]. (National Council of Teachers of Mathematics [NCTM], 2003, p. 201)

The distinguishing quality of graphs that sets them apart from other standard mathematical representations is that they are a visual medium. Although the visual aspect—the visuality—of graphs makes them an extremely rich and powerful medium for generating meaning, it is also the source of many of the incorrect responses students have to graphs. (NCTM, 2003, p. 256)

STATISTICS AND PROBABILITY PROBES

## Surveying the Prompts and Selected Responses in the Probe

The Probe consists of one math talk item. The prompts and selected responses are designed to elicit understandings and common difficulties as described below:

| If a student chooses | It is likely that the student |
|---|---|
| Olivia (correct response) | • recognizes that to accurately draw a line of best fit and to interpret the slope and the $y$-intercept, the scales of the graph need to be accurate. [See Sample Student Response 1]<br><br>*Look for indication of the student's understanding in the written explanations of how the student got the answer.* |
| McKayla | • doesn't see the error in scale but attributes the differences in equations from an error in the drawing of the line of best fit. Although the line of best fit would be different with accurate scales, this choice is usually picked by students who think the line should be a little higher based on the given graph. [See Sample Student Response 2] |
| Dylan | • attributes the difference in equations to be based on an error with data entry and not on error in scale. [See Sample Student Response 3] |

## Teaching Implications and Considerations

Ideas for eliciting more information from students about their understanding and difficulties:

- What does the $y$-intercept represent in this context? Does the $y$-intercept shown on the graph make sense?
- Are the scales of the axes accurately drawn? If not, how could you change them to make a more accurate graph?
- Would you interpret the graph differently if there was a "zigzag" line before the 10 on the $x$-axis? What does a "zigzag" line on an axis represent?
- How you would make a graph for this data? What, if any, changes would make the graph easier to read and analyze?
- Does scale affect the placement of a best-fit line? Why or why not?

Ideas for planning instruction in response to what you learned from the results of administering the Probe:

- Allow students opportunities to analyze data using various representations to allow a complete understanding of the connection between tables, graphs, equations, and the verbal description of the data.

- Have students draw and find the equations of a best-fit line using the same data but different scales. Have them compare and contrast the effects of scale changes on best-fit lines.
- Allow students to analyze and critique graphs drawn in various forms and scales.
- Provide opportunities for exploration of different slopes, *y*-intercepts, scales, and window settings to engage students in conversations on the effects each has on the appearance of graphical representations.
- Have students represent breaks in the scale using a zigzag line. Have them look at graphs to decide where and when the zigzag lines should be used.
- Explore graphical representations with a variety of technological avenues.

## Sample Student Responses to Modeling With Linear Graphs

### Responses That Suggest Understanding

*Sample Student Response 1*

Probe Item: Student chose Olivia. The *x*-axis doesn't start at 0. If the graph was drawn accurately, then it would look differently, so that would change the equation.

### Responses That Suggest Difficulty

*Sample Student Response 2*

Probe Item: Student chose McKayla. There are a lot more points above the line than below the line. If the best-fit line would have been drawn better, it would probably match the one done on the calculator.

*Sample Student Response 3*

Probe Item: Student chose Dylan. The graph shown looks fine but the data points are kinda hard to read, so they probably didn't put the right points into the calculator.

## Variation: Scatter Plots

6.1V

Determine whether the data in each scatter plot show a positive, negative, or no correlation or whether there isn't enough information to determine the correlation.

| Circle the correct answer. | Explain your choice. |
| --- | --- |
| **1.** <br> a. Positive <br> b. Negative <br> c. No correlation <br> d. Not enough information | |
| **2.** <br> a. Positive <br> b. Negative <br> c. No correlation <br> d. Not enough information | |
| **3.** <br> a. Positive <br> b. Negative <br> c. No correlation <br> d. Not enough information | |

## Comparing Data in Box Plots

Salary information was collected from employees with comparable positions at two competing companies. Thirty salaries from Company A and 30 salaries from Company B are shown in the graphs below.

Company A

Company B

Use the graphs to determine a response to each of the following statements.

| | |
|---|---|
| **1. Company B has a larger salary spread (range) than does Company A.**<br><br>True     False     Not enough information | Explain your choice: |
| **2. Q3 of Company A and the median of Company B are close to the same value.**<br><br>True     False     Not enough information | Explain your choice: |
| **3. The mean salaries of the two companies' sets are different.**<br><br>True     False     Not enough information | Explain your choice: |
| **4. Neither company has a salary that is an outlier.**<br><br>True     False     Not enough information | Explain your choice: |
| **5. Company B has more salaries in the lower two quartiles than does Company A.**<br><br>True     False     Not enough information | Explain your choice: |

## Teacher Notes: Comparing Data in Box Plots

### **Q**uestions to Consider About the Key Mathematical Concepts

When working with box plots, can students analyze and compare data sets without a given scale? To what extent do they

- make sense of analyzing and comparing two sets of five-number summaries (minimum, lower quartile, median, upper quartile, and maximum) given in box plots without a specific scale?
- reason what can or cannot be determined about data sets when given two box plots?
- describe what information is given in box plots and how that information can be used to analyze and compare two sets of data?

### Common Core Connection
### (CCSS.Math.Content.HSS-ID.A.1; CCSS.Math.Content.HSS-ID.A.2; CCSS.Math.Content.HSS-ID.A.3)

**Grade:** High School

**Domain:** Statistics and Probability

**Cluster:**

**Summarize, represent, and interpret data on a single count or measurement variable.**

A1. Represent data with plots on the real number line (dot plots, histograms, and box plots).

A2. Use statistics appropriate to the shape of the data distribution to compare center (median, mean) and spread (interquartile range, standard deviation) of two or more different data sets.

A3. Interpret differences in shape, center, and spread in the context of the data sets, accounting for possible effects of extreme data points (outliers).

### **U**ncovering Student Understanding About the Key Concepts

Using the Comparing Data in Box Plots Probe can provide the following information about how the students are thinking about information given in box plots and how to use that information to compare data sets.

| *Do they* | | *Do they* |
|---|---|---|
| • recognize spread (range) as the difference between the maximum and the minimum? | OR | • see spread (range) as where the maximum is? |
| • understand quartiles as each being 25% of the data? | OR | • look at quartiles as showing what the values of the data are? |
| • understand that the second quartile (Q2) is the median and there are an equal amount of data points above and below it? | OR | • see the middle line as representing the mean and not connected to the median? |
| • understand what an outlier is and how to find using the 1.5*IQR (interquartile range) rule and the scale increments given on a box plot? | OR | • not know what an outlier is and/or how to find one without more information given about the scale of the graph? |

## *E*xploring Excerpts From Educational Resources and Related Research

Areas of consideration:

Traditionally, statistics instruction focuses on the construction of graphs, which results in students not knowing why graphs are constructed in the first place (Friel, Curcio, & Bright, 2001). Graphs are frequently used as illustrations of data rather than as reasoning tools to learn something new in the context sphere, gain new information, or learn from the data (Wild & Pfannkuch, 1999; Konold & Pollatsek, 2002). A shifting of the instructional focus to reasoning from distributions for the purposes of making sense of data, for detecting and discovering patterns, and for unlocking the stories in the data, presents many challenges. In particular, a challenge is to understand the nature and type of reasoning involved when making informal inferences from sample distributions about population distributions. (Pfannkuch, 2006, p. 27)

Students need to make a conceptual leap to move from seeing data as an amalgam of individuals each with its own characteristics to seeing the data as an aggregate, a group with emergent properties that often are not evident in any individual member. This leap is a difficult transition. (NCTM, 2003, p. 202)

Using averages to compare two groups requires viewing averages as a way to represent or describe the entire group and not just part of it.

For this reason, Konold et al. (1997) argued that students' reluctance to use averages to compare two groups suggests that they have not developed a sense of average as a measure of a group characteristic that can be used to represent the group. (NCTM, 2003, p. 207)

## Surveying the Prompts and Selected Responses in the Probe

The Probe consists of five selected response items, each related to a common figure. The prompts and selected responses are designed to elicit understandings and common difficulties as described below:

| If a student chooses | It is likely that the student |
|---|---|
| 1. False<br><br>2. True<br><br>3. Not enough information<br><br>4. True<br><br>5. False<br><br>(correct responses) | • understands how box plots are created, what information a box plot provides about a particular data set, and what information can be gleaned about comparisons between two data sets:<br><br>  ○ For Question 1, students can use the scale increments to compare the spreads (ranges). Company A's spread goes from the 1.5th increment to the 8th, and Company B's spread goes from the 3rd increment to the 8.5th.<br>  ○ For Question 2, both are around the 6th increment.<br>  ○ For Question 3, the information given in this graph does not allow us to compare the means, only the medians.<br>  ○ For Question 4, students can use the rule for finding outliers (1.5*IQR) and the increments of the given scale. Example: Company A's interquartile range is found by subtracting Q1 from Q3. As Q3 is at the 6th increment and Q1 is at the 3rd, the IQR is 3 increments. Multiply this by 1.5, and it is 4.5 increments. This can be added to Q3 or subtracted from Q1 to see if any data points lie beyond these increments.<br>  ○ For Question 5, as there are 30 salaries represented in each company, each has the same amount in the lower 50%.<br><br>[See Sample Student Responses 1 and 2]<br><br>*Look for indication of the student's understanding in the written explanations of how the student got the answer.* |
| 1. True or Not enough information | • does not understand how to find information about comparing two spreads (ranges) without specific scale values given or misinterprets Company B's higher maximum with a larger spread. [See Sample Student Response 3] |

*(Continued)*

(Continued)

| If a student chooses | It is likely that the student |
|---|---|
| 2. False or Not enough information | • does not know what Q3 and/or the median is and/or where to find them on the box plots. Often students think that a specific scale needs to be given in order to compare these measures. [See Sample Student Response 4] |
| 3. True or False | • does not know which measure of center is given in a box plot or does not have an understanding of how the median and/or mean is found. [See Sample Student Response 3] |
| 4. False or Not enough information | • does not know what an outlier is or how to use a box plot without scale values to determine if there are outliers. Some students will answer True for this but will not have a complete justification and instead write that it "looks like" there is not an outlier. [See Sample Student Response 4] |
| 5. True or Not enough information | • equates the larger lower box in Company B (Q1 to the median) as having more salaries that fall between the quartiles. [See Sample Student Response 5] |

## Teaching Implications and Considerations

Ideas for eliciting more information from students about their understanding and difficulties:

- How many "sections" are there in a box plot? What does each section represent?
- Why are the sections different sizes? Does this mean there are different amounts of data in each section?
- What information about a data set is included in a five-number summary?
- What is a quartile? What are some other names for quartiles? How are quartiles found? Are quartiles always a value in the data set? When are they? When are they not?
- Are the mean and the median the same value? How are each found? Are the mean and median always a value in the data set? When are they? When are they not?
- How do you tell if there are outliers? What is the IQR (interquartile range)? How do you use the IQR to find outliers?
- How can the increments of the scale on the graph be used to find the IQR?
- Do we always need to consider outliers when analyzing data?

Ideas for planning instruction in response to what you learned from the results of administering the Probe:

- When analyzing data, provide many opportunities and contexts in which to do so. Having students collect their own data is a great way for them to have a connection with the analysis.
- Motivate students by encouraging them to ask and explore questions of personal interest to them. Encourage them to include questions about the data as a whole and not individual data values.
- Use different graphing tools to represent data in a variety of ways, comparing and contrasting each for pros and cons.
- Have students represent data on a box plot, a histogram, a pie chart (circle graph), and so on to see what each type of graph is best used for and what kind of information each type of graph shows.
- Students should explore changes in scale to see the visual changes in graphical representation.
- Have group and classroom discussions on measures of center and spread.
- Have students discuss mean and median and find data in which one is a better average than another.
- Allow students to explore how newspapers, magazines, advertisements, and so on misrepresent data by using graphs and statistical measures. This allows them to look at data and representations with a critical eye.

## Sample Student Responses to Comparing Data in Box Plots

### Responses That Suggest Understanding

*Sample Student Response 1*

Probe Item 1: Student chose False. The maximum is higher in Company B but the spread is bigger for Company A as the max and min are farther apart.

Probe Item 2: Student chose True. Both are around the 6th tic mark.

Probe Item 3: Student chose Not enough information. I don't think you can tell where the mean is on a box plot without more information about it. The middle lines are the median, though.

Probe Item 5: Student chose False. As they both have 30 salaries, there is the same number of salaries from 0 to the $\frac{1}{2}$ way mark (lower two quartiles).

*Sample Student Response 2*

Probe Item 4: Student chose True. You can kind of tell by looking but we are supposed to multiply 1.5 times the IQR. At first I didn't think it could be done, but then I decided to put my own numbers on the tic marks, starting with 1 and going to 9. This let me find the IQR of A and B to be both around 4.5 tic marks. I then added this to Q3 . . . no outliers!

*(Continued)*

(Continued)

**Responses That Suggest Difficulty**

*Sample Student Response 3*

Probe Item 1: Student chose True. Company B's biggest value is a little higher than A's.

Probe Item 3: Student chose True. They cannot be the same with the data so different.

*Sample Student Response 4*

Probe Item 2: Student chose Not enough information. We are not given any information about specific salaries so we cannot tell.

Probe Item 4: Student chose Not enough information. There is not enough information for this one either. You cannot find the IQR so cannot really tell.

*Sample Student Response 5*

Probe Item 5: Student chose Yes. The first part of the box in B is a lot bigger than the first part of the box in A.

## Variation: Comparing Data in Box Plots

Salary information was collected from employees with comparable positions at two competing companies. Thirty salaries from Company A and 30 salaries from Company B are shown in the graphs below.

Company A

Company B

Use the graphs to determine a response to each of the following statements.

| | Explain your choice: |
|---|---|
| **1. Company B has a larger salary spread (range) than does Company A.**<br><br>True    False    Not enough information | |
| **2. Q3 of Company A and the median of Company B are close to the same value.**<br><br>True    False    Not enough information | Explain your choice: |
| **3. The mean salaries of the two companies' sets are different.**<br><br>True    False    Not enough information | Explain your choice: |
| **4. Neither company has a salary that is an outlier.**<br><br>True    False    Not enough information | Explain your choice: |
| **5. Company B has more salaries in the lower two quartiles than does Company A.**<br><br>True    False    Not enough information | Explain your choice: |

## Probability

6.3

| Determine the response that shows how to solve the problem. | Justify your choice. |
|---|---|
| 1. A jar contains 6 red balls, 3 green balls, 5 white balls, and 7 yellow balls. Two balls are chosen from the jar with replacement. What is the probability of choosing a red and a yellow?<br><br>a. $\dfrac{6}{21} \cdot \dfrac{7}{20}$     c. $\dfrac{6}{21} + \dfrac{7}{20}$<br><br>b. $\dfrac{6}{21} \cdot \dfrac{7}{21}$     d. $\dfrac{6}{21} + \dfrac{7}{21}$ | |
| 2. A day of the week is chosen at random. What is the probability of choosing a Monday or a Wednesday?<br><br>a. $\dfrac{1}{7} \cdot \dfrac{1}{7}$     c. $\dfrac{1}{7} + \dfrac{1}{7}$<br><br>b. $\dfrac{1}{7} \cdot \dfrac{1}{6}$     d. $\dfrac{1}{7} + \dfrac{1}{6}$ | |
| 3. Two cards are chosen at random from a deck of 52 cards without replacement. What is the probability of choosing two Aces?<br><br>a. $\dfrac{4}{52} \cdot \dfrac{3}{52}$     c. $\dfrac{4}{52} + \dfrac{4}{51}$<br><br>b. $\dfrac{4}{52} \cdot \dfrac{3}{51}$     d. $\dfrac{4}{52} + \dfrac{3}{51}$ | |

## Teacher Notes: Probability

### Questions to Consider About the Key Mathematical Concepts

When working with probability problems, do students recognize when to apply addition or multiplication rules? To what extent do they

- recognize events as being independent or dependent?
- reason how likely it is that something will happen and whether to use addition or multiplication to find the probability of a situation?
- describe the event(s) using the language of probability and describe the process of computing the probabilities?

### Common Core Connection (CCSS.Math.Content.HSS-CP.A.2)

**Grade:** High School

**Domain:** Statistics and Probability

**Cluster:**

**Understand independence and conditional probability and use them to interpret data.**

A2. Understand that two events $A$ and $B$ are independent if the probability of $A$ and $B$ occurring together is the product of their probabilities, and use this characterization to determine if they are independent.

### Common Core Connection (CCSS.Math.Content.HSS-CP.B.7)

**Grade:** High School

**Domain:** Statistics and Probability

**Cluster:**

**Use the rules of probability to compute probabilities of compound events.**

B7. Apply the Addition Rule, $P(A \text{ or } B) = P(A) + P(B) - P(A \text{ and } B)$, and interpret the answer in terms of the model.

### Uncovering Student Understanding About the Key Concepts

Using the Probability Probe can provide the following information about how the students are thinking about compound probabilities.

*Do they*

- understand that events can be independent or dependent on other events?

OR

- look for words and/or phrases in descriptions of probability situations to decide when to use addition or multiplication rules?

OR

- understand the difference between situations with replacement and without replacement?

OR

*Do they*

- not distinguish the difference between independent/dependent events?

- misinterpret descriptions or not know when to use addition or multiplication in probability problems?

- not see replacement, or lack of, as a necessary part of the solution process?

# Exploring Excerpts From Educational Resources and Related Research

Areas of consideration:

Both psychological and mathematical conceptions interfere when students are asked questions that involve compound probability. Compound probability problems can involve conjunctions in which the events are independent on one another or in which the events are dependent on one another. . . . Students have difficulty just sorting out the mathematics of whether events are statistically dependent or independent in probability problems. (NCTM, 2003, p. 221)

[Tversky and Kahneman (1983)] found that the bias toward the conjunction fallacy—thinking that compound events are more likely to occur than simple events—is very robust across many different scenarios. (NCTM, 2003, p. 221)

In the case of teaching conditional probability, the literature bears out the importance of taking learner characteristics into account in designing instruction. Probability appears to be one of the most difficult mathematical subjects to learn, as numerous misconceptions have been cataloged by researchers (Shaughnessy, 1992). In the case of conditional probability, one such misconception is that "mutually exclusive events" are the same as "independent events" (Kelly & Zwiers, 1986). Another misconception is that all conditional probability situations must involve sequential events (Ancker, 2006). Students might also incorrectly equate the concepts of conditionality and causality (Falk, 1986). To build learner-centered environments, teachers must become aware of and address such aspects of students' knowledge and beliefs. (Groth, 2010, p. 36)

Although the most obvious application of probability in the world around us occurs in games of chance, probability actually plays an important role in daily life. We use it to make decisions in such diverse fields as weather forecasting, military operations, business predictions, insurance calculations, and the design and quality control of consumer products. The study of probability also helps students build skills for informal decision making. Simply recognizing that insurance rates are substantially higher for teenage drivers (and, in particular, for male teenage drivers) may help students understand how probability directly affects their lives. (Schwols & Dempsey, 2012, p. 119)

## **S**urveying the Prompts and Selected Responses in the Probe

The Probe consists of three separate selected response items. The prompts and selected responses are designed to elicit understandings and common difficulties as described below:

| If a student chooses | It is likely that the student |
|---|---|
| 1. b<br>(correct response) | • understands that the probability of two independent events (because of replacement) can be found by computing the probability of each event separately and then multiplying the results together. The key words/phrases in the problem are *and* and *with replacement*. [See Sample Student Response 1]<br><br>*Look for indication of the student's understanding in the written explanations of how the student got the answer.* |
| 2. c<br>(correct response) | • understands this problem to be about two mutually exclusive events. The probability of Monday or Wednesday being chosen is the sum of the probabilities of each event. The key word is *or* in the problem. [See Sample Student Response 1] |
| 3. b<br>(correct response) | • understands how to find the conditional probability of an event in relationship to a prior event already having occurred. The first event has the probability of 4 aces out of 52, but for the second event there would only be 3 aces left out of 51 cards because the first ace would not have been replaced. The key words/phrases in the problem are *without replacement*, and *and* is implied. [See Sample Student Response 2] |

*(Continued)*

(Continued)

| If a student chooses | It is likely that the student |
|---|---|
| Various other responses | • does not understand key descriptive words or phrases that determine how to find probabilities (see above for descriptions). Students often confuse when to add or multiply when finding probabilities. They also often misunderstand and/or confuse "replacement" and "without replacement" situations. [See Sample Student Responses 3 and 4] |

## Teaching Implications and Considerations

Ideas for eliciting more information from students about their understanding and difficulties:

- What is the sample space for each of the events?
- How many events are there in each problem? Describe the events (compound, independent, dependent, mutually exclusive, with/without replacement, etc.).
- Are there events that are more likely to occur than others? How will probability reflect that?
- What are some key words or phrases that would help to decide whether to add or multiply the separate events?

Ideas for planning instruction in response to what you learned from the results of administering the Probe:

- Students explore topics in descriptive statistics in middle school (Grade 8), but most students have not worked with probability since Grade 7 (Schwols & Dempsey, 2012, p. 119). A review of basic probability would be a good starting point for most high school students.
- Use experiments, data collection, and simulations as tools in probability instruction. Students generally enjoy testing out their ideas and guesses to see how accurate they are.
- Allow students time to explore their own methods and strategies of solving probability problems before showing them formal ones.
- "Students need more experience building sample spaces and more experience listing the set of all possible outcomes in probability experiments" (NCTM, 2003, p. 222).
- Focus beginning lessons on sample space in different types of situations so students can begin to distinguish between dependent and independent events.
- Help students develop a deeper understanding of the extensive ways probability is used by including a variety of real-word situations (including collecting their own data and computer simulations).

"There are ever-increasing applications and uses of probability and statistics in business and industry. Informed citizens need to be numerate in data and chance and need to know how to decipher and make sense out of information that is presented in newspapers, medical reports, consumer reports, and environmental studies" (NCTM, 2003, p. 223).

- "Make connections between probability and statistics. In particular, connect the notion of sample space in probability with the concept of variation in statistics. Introduce probability *through* data; start with statistics to get to probability" (NCTM, 2003, p. 224).

## Sample Student Responses to Probability

### Responses That Suggest Understanding

*Sample Student Response 1*

Probe Item 1: Student chose b. This is a multiplication problem because of the word *and*. As there is replacement, both denominators would be 21 because there are 21 balls total. The probability of getting a red is $\frac{6}{21}$, and the probability of getting a yellow is $\frac{7}{21}$. Multiply those together and you have your answer.

Probe Item 2: Student chose c. This is an addition problem (*or*), and as the days of the week are not dependent (mutually exclusive) on each other, the denominators would both be 7 (7 days in a week). Monday is $\frac{1}{7}$, and Wednesday is $\frac{1}{7}$ too. Add them up.

*Sample Student Response 2*

Probe Item 3: Student chose b. It states no replacement so the second choice would have one less card (51 instead of 52). There are 4 aces in first choice $\left(\frac{4}{52}\right)$ and 3 in second $\left(\frac{3}{51}\right)$. I multiplied because it could be written "What is the probability of choosing an ace and an ace?"

### Responses That Suggest Difficulty

*Sample Student Response 3*

Probe Item 2: Student chose d. The probability of choosing a red is $\frac{6}{21}$, and the probability of choosing a yellow is $\frac{7}{21}$. Add these two probabilities up and you have your answer.

*Sample Student Response 4*

Probe Item 3: Student chose c. Because there is no replacement, the first one is 4 out of 52 $\left(\frac{4}{52}\right)$ and the second one is 4 out of 51 $\left(\frac{4}{51}\right)$, so these would be the two probabilities we would be working with.

# 7

# Additional Considerations

An assessment activity can help learning if it provides information that teachers and their students can use as feedback in assessing themselves and one another and in modifying the teaching and learning activities in which they are engaged. (Black, Harrison, Lee, Marshall, & Wiliam, 2004, p. 10)

**M**athematics assessment Probes represent an approach to diagnostic assessment. They can be used for formative assessment purposes if the information about students' understandings and misunderstandings is used in a way that moves students' learning forward. There is a wide range of considerations in this chapter, including using the Probes to

- establish learning targets,
- allow for individual reflection,
- give student interviews,
- address individual needs,
- promote mathematical discourse,
- support the mathematical practices, and
- build capacity among teachers within and across courses.

Since the first *Uncovering Student Thinking* resource was in development, we have worked with and learned from the many teachers who have implemented our assessment Probes or have developed their own assessment Probes to use in their classrooms. Observing classes, trying out strategies ourselves with students, and listening to teachers describe their experiences and approaches have helped us capture various images from practice over time. The vignettes that accompany each of the considerations are chosen to highlight features of a particular instructional approach.

# ESTABLISHING LEARNING TARGETS

Stating and sharing intended outcomes of learning and assessment is really the foundation for all formative assessment activities. (Wylie et al., 2012, p. 22)

Establishing learning targets and sharing criteria for success in meeting the target is the foundation of the embedded formative assessment process (Council of Chief State School Officers [CCSSO], 2008; Heritage, 2010, Moss & Brookhart, 2012; Wiliam, 2011; Wylie et al., 2012). The need to develop students' content knowledge, including knowledge of the important mathematics concepts, procedures, and skills outlined in the Common Core Mathematical Standards and Practices, is a priority for mathematics educators. In order for students to meet these established expectations, instruction and assessment must take place with a clear learning target in mind. Standards should inform teachers' thinking about learning targets as an interconnected cluster of learning goals that develop over time. By clarifying the specific ideas and skills described in the standards and articulating them as specific lesson-level learning targets aligned to criteria for success, teachers are in a better position to uncover the gap between students' existing knowledge or skill and the knowledge or skill described in the learning target and criteria for success.

## Assessment Probe Use Related to Learning Targets

Each assessment Probe addresses a key mathematical idea aligned to a Common Core mathematics content standard(s), providing an example of how subsets of mathematics standards can be developed as learning goals. The example in Figure 7.1, from the Transformation of Functions Probe, highlights two components of the Teacher Notes helpful in determining learning targets: Questions to Consider About the Key Mathematic Concepts and the connections to the Common Core State Standards for Mathematics.

Many teachers we work with are establishing learning targets on a daily basis and are using the Probes as tools to both support the development of a learning target prior to a lesson and help students reach the learning target during a lesson.

When using a Probe to support the development of a learning target prior to a lesson, teachers give the Probe to students one to three days prior to the upcoming lesson or unit of instruction. They analyze the evidence gathered from the assessment to gauge students' current understandings and misunderstandings and use this information to develop a learning target or set of learning targets.

**Figure 7.1** Excerpts From Teacher Notes for Transformations of Functions

## Questions to Consider About the Key Mathematical Concepts

When working with functions, do students understand how algebraic representations describe graphical transformations? To what extent do they

- make sense of various forms of algebraic representations and correctly relate it to a graphical transformation?
- reason about the algebraic and graphical connections?
- describe graphical effects of various algebraic transformations?

### Common Core Connection (CCSS.Math.Content.HSF-BF.B.3)

**Grade:** High School

**Domain:** Functions

**Cluster:**

**Build new functions from existing functions.**

B3. Identify the effect on the graph of replacing $f(x)$ by $f(x) + k$, $k\,f(x)$, $f(kx)$, and $f(x + k)$ for specific values of $k$ (both positive and negative); find the value of $k$ given the graphs. Experiment with cases and illustrate an explanation of the effects on the graph using technology. Include recognizing even and odd functions from their graphs and algebraic expressions for them.

The following image from practice provides an example of using a Probe prior to the start of a lesson or set of lessons.

About three-quarters way through the unit, I gave the Matrices Probe variation to determine the extent to which my students were beginning to generalize from examples and nonexamples the various properties of matrix operations. I gave the Probe as an exit ticket and sorted the responses to get a sense of the class. I started with #1 and first quickly sorted the papers into two piles, true and false. From there I quickly sorted those with False into three categories, those who had solid justifications, those whose justifications didn't provide evidence of solid understanding, and those whose justifications showed evidence of correct response for an incorrect reason. I also sorted those with True into two categories, those whose justifications showed some correct reasoning and those who showed the overgeneralization from number properties that all multiplication is commutative (see Figure 7.2).

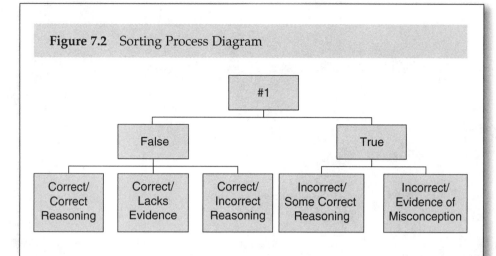

**Figure 7.2** Sorting Process Diagram

After making some notes about the data, I continued working through the other problems using a similar process. After determining that more than half of the class either had incorrect reasoning or insufficient evidence on each of the problems, I decided on the following learning goal for the next lesson:

**Learning Target:** How matrix properties are similar to and different from rational numbers properties.

**Success Criterion 1:** Use matrix properties to justify statements that are true.

**Success Criterion 2:** Use a counterexample to justify a false statement.

To help students meet these criteria, I created and used a series of four short activities using examples and nonexamples, technology, and readings related to the statements included in the Teacher Notes.

When using a Probe as a tool *within* a lesson or set of lessons, teachers first establish an alignment between the Probe content and the established learning target. In addition, they design instructional activities to support predicted understandings and misunderstandings likely to be uncovered by the Probe.

Prior to working on a unit on cross sections, I planned a lesson on classification of three-dimensional figures. I designed the lesson to first introduce/review the different definitions of the figures. Showing various shapes and names, students were asked to work in groups to determine if the name matched the shape and why. After the group activity, students completed the Names of the Shape Probe (see page 147) individually. I projected the following information (see Figure 7.3) for Problem 1 on my smartboard.

(Continued)

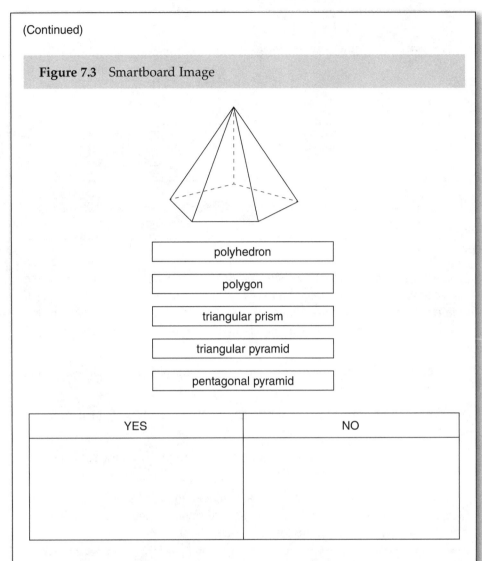

**Figure 7.3**   Smartboard Image

| polyhedron |
| polygon |
| triangular prism |
| triangular pyramid |
| pentagonal pyramid |

| YES | NO |
|---|---|
|  |  |

As students were completing the Probe, I surveyed their responses for correct and incorrect selections to predetermine who I would ask to place a particular shape name in one of the columns on the board. My goal was to have a mixture of correct and incorrect placements after students moved a name to either the Yes or No column. All names were placed in one of the columns before asking for feedback from the whole class. Volunteers chose a name and provided justification for whether the name should remain where it was originally placed or whether the name should be moved to the other column. After all names where correctly placed and I was satisfied with the justifications, we moved on to Problem 2, continuing the process for all three problems.

As the final step, I asked the students to revise their probe based on the class discussion. All students were required to revise not only their answer selections as needed but also their explanations.

# INDIVIDUAL METACOGNITION AND REFLECTION (THE 4CS)

The Conceptual Change Model begins with having students become aware of their own thinking. Through a series of developmental steps, it helps them to confront their views and to refine them if necessary, then to immediately use their new understanding. (Stepans et al., 2005, p. 37)

The conceptual change model as described by Stepans and colleagues (2005) takes into consideration recommendations from research and is rooted in the learning cycle approach. The goal of the conceptual change model is to uncover students' current ideas about a topic before teaching new content related to the topic. Students learn by integrating new knowledge with what they already know and can do. Sometimes this new knowledge is integrated in a way that contributes to or builds on an existing misunderstanding. Through the conceptual change approach, since ideas are elicited prior to instruction, existing preconceptions and/or misconconceptions can be confronted explicitly, minimizing situations in which students are trying to integrate new knowledge into a flawed or underdeveloped framework of ideas. This explicit confrontation of preconceptions or misconceptions creates cognitive dissonance in which students begin to question and rethink their preconceptions, and further instruction and reflection can now help students understand the new concept. Our 4Cs model, an adaptation of the conceptual change model, consists of four stages, as shown in Figure 7.4.

**Figure 7.4**   The 4Cs Model

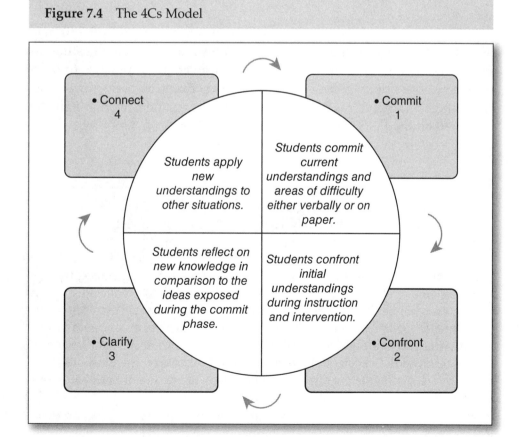

*Source:* Rose Tobey and Fagan (2013).

At this point, you may be wondering how the 4Cs model connects with the QUEST Cycle. The QUEST Cycle is written from a teacher point of view and implicitly incorporates the 4Cs model. Since even the most effective teachers cannot do the actual learning for their students, the 4Cs model provides the critical student perspective.

## Assessment Probe Use Related to the 4Cs Model

Teachers using the 4Cs model in conjunction with assessment Probes typically use the following process:

1. *Commit.* Choose a Probe to elicit ideas related to a learning target. Give the Probe to all students, capturing student responses by asking them to write explanations, scripting their explanations, or a combination of both.
2. *Confront.* Provide instruction based on results, integrating a variety of anonymous student responses, both correct and incorrect, into the lesson at appropriate junctures and lead class discussion about the responses.
3. *Clarify.* Return students' initial responses to the Probe to them (or read them to students) and ask students to clarify or revise anything in the response based on what they just learned in the lesson.
4. *Connect.* Pose additional questions similar to those in the Probe to assess whether students have met the learning target.

The image above about using the Names of the Shape Probe to help students meet the learning target provides one image of engaging students in the 4Cs model. In Chapter 1, we used an image from practice to illustrate how assessment Probes can create a link between assessment, instruction, and learning. We remind you of that image here to highlight an additional example of the 4Cs model.

In a high school geometry class, students first complete the Is It a Parallelogram? Probe individually. Next, small groups of students discuss and reconcile their different ideas about whether the information provided about a figure is sufficient to determine whether that figure is a parallelogram. With the goal of consensus, students within each group justify their choice, trying to persuade others who disagree. As each group works to produce justifications that will be shared with the whole class, the teacher circulates among the group, probing further and encouraging argumentation. At the end of class, students are asked to revisit their initial responses and are provided time to revise their choices and explanations. The teacher uses this information to prepare for the next day's lesson (excerpt adapted from Keeley & Rose Tobey, 2011).

# GIVING STUDENT INTERVIEWS

Whenever we try to get at a student's thinking, we should try to focus not only on what the student is thinking but also on what the student understands about his or her own knowledge. The questions we ask when interviewing a student will help the student become more aware of her own cognitive processes. (Ashlock, 2006, p. 27)

Conducting individual or small group interviews provides information beyond what written student work can provide. Interviewing students offers insight into their level of understanding and their ability to put mathematical ideas into words and/or representations. The interview process also allows teachers to gather information about the range of learning needs within a group of students. Teachers who regularly incorporate student interviews selectively interview a subset of students or all of their students depending on how they wish to use the results.

## Assessment Probe Use Related to Student Interviews

Good interviewing requires careful preparation in advance, keeping in mind purposes, method of selection, environment, questions and follow-up probes, and uses. (Stepans et al., 2005, p. 277)

Teachers have found that any Probe can be administered as an interview and they see benefits to this mode of administration at any age.

Many teachers manage individual interviews by conducting them while the students not being interviewed are engaged in other activities. Teachers can also capitalize on a small-group approach to "interview" multiple students individually as they simultaneously work on the tasks of the Probe. When managed well, these conversations provide valuable information about students' thinking and their ability to build on the ideas of other students to advance their thinking. One challenge of the small-group interview approach is the temptation to jump from information gathering to instruction. Stay focused on and be explicit with students that the goal of this small group activity is for you to listen to their ideas and ask questions in order to plan for a new learning experience on another day. Being explicit in this way avoids confusion for students who may also participate in small intervention groups or other small-group work focused on instruction.

# ADDRESSING INDIVIDUAL NEEDS

Although many teachers feel they lack the time or tools to pre-assess on a regular basis, the data derived from pre-assessment are essential in driving differentiated instruction. (Small, 2009, p. 5)

In addition to using Probes as preassessment, understanding how the math content contained in the Probe connects to a progression of math learning can support efforts to differentiate instruction to meet students' needs:

> The Common Core State Standards in mathematics were built on progressions: narrative documents describing the progression of a topic across a number of grade levels, informed both by research on children's cognitive development and by the logical structure of mathematics. These documents were spliced together and then sliced into grade level standards. From that point on the work focused on refining and revising the grade level standards. The early drafts of the progressions documents no longer correspond to the current state of the standards.
>
> It is important to produce up-to-date versions of the progressions documents. They can explain why standards are sequenced the way they are, point out cognitive difficulties and pedagogical solutions, and give more detail on particularly knotty areas of the mathematics. (Institute for Mathematics and Education [IME], 2012)

Being aware of and understanding a progression of learning of a topic is important when considering how to address the needs of students. Often individual students can be grouped with others who have a similar misunderstanding or who have a similar missing foundational concept that is posing a barrier to learning the mathematics of the learning target. Compiling an inventory for a set of papers can provide a sense of the class' progress and thus inform decisions about how to differentiate instruction. Decisions about next steps should be informed based on the goal of moving students' understanding toward a defined learning target: when the gap between existing knowledge and the learning target is too great, however, students may need to access the content at a "lower" point in the learning progression. This may require developing alternate and additional learning targets, allowing students to build the necessary prerequisite understanding. Probes provide critical information to inform these decisions and are therefore a useful tool for all teachers of math, including special educators, Title I teachers, and interventionists.

## PROMOTING MATHEMATICAL DISCOURSE

> Because discussions help students to summarize and synthesize the mathematics they are learning, the use of student thinking is a critical element of mathematical discourse. When teachers help students build on their thinking through talk, misconceptions are made clearer to both teacher and student, and at the same time, conceptual and procedural knowledge deepens. (Garcia, 2012, p. 3)

> Talking the talk is an important part of learning. (Black & Harrison, 2004, p. 4)

When students are talking about their mathematical ideas—whether in a whole-class discussion, in small groups, or in pairs—they are using the language and conventions of mathematics.

Students primarily learn vocabulary indirectly through their conversations with others and from the books, programs, and information they are exposed to from the Internet. However, because many words used in mathematics may not come up in everyday contexts—and if they do, they may mean something totally different—math vocabulary needs to be explicitly taught. Students' use of math terms is directly related to their experiences. Lack of exposure to math situations and opportunities to develop a correct mathematical vocabulary can deprive students of the language of math. The language of math is specific and uses words to denote not only meaning but also symbolic notation. Symbols enable mathematical ideas to be expressed in precise ways that reflect quantitative relationships. Misunderstandings about the meaning of a math symbol or notation or how to use it can affect understanding. Just as some words can take on different meanings in different contexts, so can some mathematical symbols.

## Assessment Probe Use Related to Promoting Mathematical Discourse

The classroom images used in this chapter illustrate how a teacher can use the Probes to engage students in discussion. The book, *Mathematics Formative Assessment: 75 Practical Strategies for Linking Assessment, Instruction and Learning* (Keeley & Rose Tobey, 2011), provides descriptions of specific strategies that can be combined with assessment Probes to promote learning through mathematical discourse. Many of these strategies have been used or modified for use in conjunction with Probes. Two such strategies, Agreement Circles and the more commonly used Think-Pair-Share, provide a whole-group strategy example and a pair/small-group example of promoting learning through discourse.

### Agreement Circles

Agreement Circles provide a kinesthetic way to activate thinking and engage students in discussing and defending their mathematical ideas. Students stand in a large circle as the teacher reads a statement. The students who agree with the statement step to the center of the circle. Those who disagree remain standing on the outside of the circle. Those in the inner circle face their peers still standing around the outside circle and then divide themselves into small groups of students who agree and disagree. The small groups then engage in discussion to defend their thinking. This is repeated with several rounds of statements relating to the same topic, each time with students starting by standing around the large circle. At the beginning, this strategy works best with Probes that generated substantial disagreement. Over time, once the classroom environment allows for students to take risks and feel safe doing so, the strategy can be successfully used when a smaller range of students choose certain selected responses. (Keeley & Rose Tobey, 2011, pp. 54–55)

### *Think-Square-Share*

Think-Pair-Share begins by providing students with an opportunity to activate their own thinking. The pairing strategy allows students to first share their ideas with one other person and modify their ideas or construct new knowledge as they interact with their partner. Typically, students are next asked to share ideas with a larger group. By having had a chance to discuss their ideas with another student as a pair, many students are more comfortable and willing to respond to the whole group discussion, Hence the Think-Square-Share approach. As a result of discussing ideas with another pair, the quality of responses often improves and contributes to a higher quality whole group discussion as well. Thoughtful pairing of students helps to ensure that the pair conversation is productive. Consider pairing students with others whom they will engage productively and whose content level understanding is similar enough for common ground yet reflects differences that will evoke conversation.

In a Think-Square-Share variation, students begin discussions in groups of four rather than in pairs. When using a Probe with selected response choices, teachers can prearrange groups so that each includes students who chose different selections. In their "square," they have a opportunity to discuss their thinking and try to justify their reasoning or modify it based on information they gain from the discussion. (Keeley & Rose Tobey, 2011, pp. 189–190)

## SUPPORTING THE MATHEMATICAL PRACTICES

Formative assessment begins by identifying a learning goal, based on a course standard from the Common Core State Standards (CCSS). Since the course standards in the Common Core State Standards for Mathematics (CCSSM) "define what students should understand and be able to do," it is important for teachers to find out what students know and can do both conceptually and procedurally in relation to the expectation for learning. In addition to these content standards, an important feature of the CCSSM is the Standards for Mathematical Practices. These practices describe a variety of processes and proficiencies that teachers at all grade levels should seek to develop in their students. Since the CCSSM does not define the methods and strategies used to determine the readiness and prior knowledge necessary to achieve the standards, the mathematics assessment Probes in this book complement the CCSSM's eight Standards for Mathematical Practices and their link to mathematical content.

How the use of Probes supports each of the practice clusters (see Appendix B for more information about these clusters) is described next, beginning with the practices related to reasoning and explanation.

## Assessment Probe Use Related to the Reasoning and Explaining Practice Cluster

Simply using the mathematics assessment Probes with students will not result in students who are proficient within this cluster of practices. Instead, use of the Probes over time, combined with higher expectations for reasons and justification for selecting a response, will support students as they progress toward proficiency. Use of the follow-up questions accompanying the Probes (see Figure 7.5 for an example) can help students who are having difficulty describing their reasoning or who give only brief explanations such as "I just knew" or "I learned that in algebra last year."

**Figure 7.5**  Solving Quadratic Equations Follow-Up Questions

### *T*eaching Implications and Considerations

Ideas for eliciting more information from students about their understanding and difficulties:

- For students having difficulty with factoring, ask, "What solution methods might help you determine the types of solutions?"
- For students who apply the quadratic formula, ask, "How might you determine whether the solutions are real or complex without finding the actual solutions?"
- For students who are only looking at the form of the equation, ask, "How can this equation be written in a different form?"
- Ask the student to graph the equation and compare the results.

Since students naturally generalize from examples and nonexamples, some of the assessment Probes are structured or can be structured as card sorts, which capitalize on examples and nonexamples to help students build important reasoning skills. It is expected that high school students are able to use a variety of ways to justify their answers, including generating and organizing data to make, validate, or refute a conjecture and developing facility with inductive and deductive reasoning. The extent to which students are able to use these skills when giving explanations can be elicited through use of the Probes.

Some of the assessment Probes make use of the "math-talk" structure in which students are asked to decide who they agree with and provide a reason for their choice. Probes that are structured in this way provide opportunities for students to critique the reasonableness of another's answer and to justify their conclusions. Again, using Probes structured in this way only on occasion during the school year will not build students' ability in a meaningful way. Instead, students will need multiple opportunities over the course of the school year and across all of the mathematics domains to build these abilities:

> When students derive answers to problems, we not only need to get at their thinking in order to understand how they obtained those answers, we also need to learn how they justify their answers—how they prove they are correct in their own thinking. We can look for three kinds of justification schemes identified by Sowder and Harel and illustrated by Flores:
>
> - *Externally based schemes* in which a textbook or authority figure is cited as justification
> - *Empirically based schemes* in which students use perception or concrete objects to show that their answer is correct
> - *Analysis use schemes* in which students use strategies or state mathematical relations to justify their answer.
>
> As a student's thinking develops over time, we expect to see fewer uses of justification schemes that are externally based. We even hope to see use of empirically-based schemes eventually give way to schemes that use analysis, for such thinking is distinctly mathematical. (Ashlock, 2006, p. 28)

In summary, high school students in all courses should be encouraged to make conjectures, be given time to search for evidence to prove or disprove those conjectures using inductive and deductive reasoning, and be expected to explain and justify their ideas. Students should be introduced to and be expected to use basic logic words in their explanation, including *if . . . , then . . . , and, or, not, all,* and *some, and to* incorporate mathematical properties and relationships, rather than authority (e.g., because I read that in my textbook), as the basis for the argument.

## Assessment Probe Use Related to the Seeing Structure and Generalizing Practice Cluster

Many of the mathematics targets of the assessment Probes align to the CCSSM content standards directly associated with the Seeing Structure and Generalizing Practice Structure. Students should spend time studying functions within a family, varying parameters to develop an understanding of how the parameters affect the graph of a function and its key features (Common Core Standards Writing Team, 2013b, p. 9). Consistent with the practice of looking for and making use of structure, students should also develop the practice of writing expressions for functions in ways that reveal the key features of the function (Common Core Standards Writing Team, 2013b, p. 10). The Equation of the Function Probe (see Figure 7.6) elicits from students whether they have generalized the relationships between representations of exponential graphs and equations.

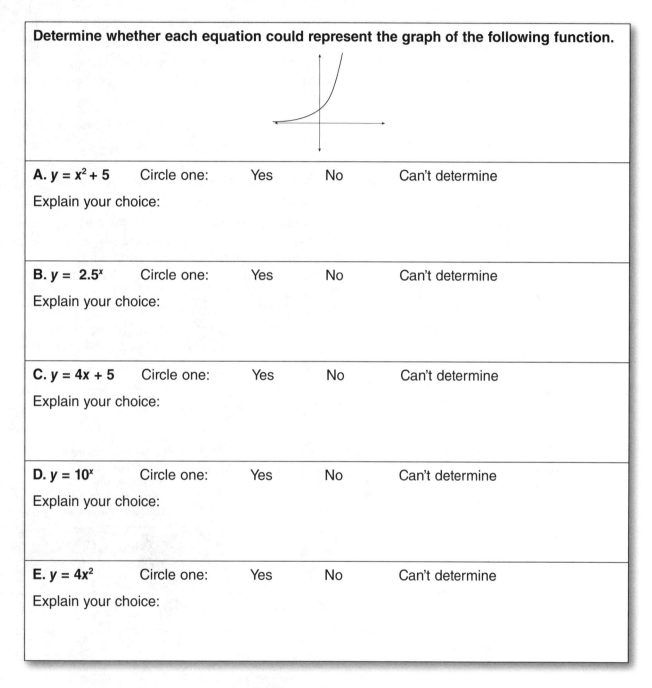

**Figure 7.6** Equation of the Function Probe

Students who are able to choose the correct responses are likely to be generalizing about the graph and equations. The Level 2 explanation is key to determining whether, in fact, students are using these generalizations and are able to explain or articulate the reasons for their correct responses. A solid explanation showcases the student's recognition of the key features of exponential functions when written in algebraic form by looking for relevant information shown in the graph that will help determine possible equations without knowing the scale of the graph.

### Assessment Probe Use Related to the Modeling and Using Tools Practice Cluster

Many of the mathematical targets of the assessment Probes align to the Common Core content standards directly associated with the Modeling and Using Tools Practice Cluster. The Equation of the Function Probe (see Figure 7.6) requires students to understand how exponential growth can be represented by a graph and an equation. In another example, the Modeling With Linear Graphs Probe (see Figure 7.7) requires students to model a given situation with an equation.

**Figure 7.7**   Modeling With Linear Graphs Probe

## Modeling With Linear Graphs

The following graph shows data that a group of students found on ice cream sales in dollars (*y* values) versus temperature in °C (*x* values). They drew a best-fit line and found the equation of the line to be $y = 19.5x + 100$. When the same data were entered into a graphing calculator and a regression model found, the equation was $y = 30x - 159.5$. Why is the best-fit equation so different from the regression model?

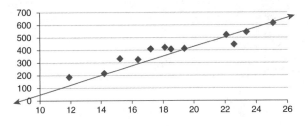

I think it is different because they did not find the best-fit line.

McKayla

I think it is different because their graph does not show all of the *x* intervals.

Olivia

I think it is different because they probably didn't put the data into the calculator accurately.

Dylan

Who do you agree with and why?

Modeling a relationship between two quantities using a line of best fit requires that students are able to reason about features of the graph and how best to "place" the line. Once again, it is the elaboration prompt that requires students to describe their choice and allows the teacher to get a better sense of the students' reasoning.

In addition to Probes that are directly connected to content standards related to modeling and/or the use of tools, all the assessment Probes have the ability to elicit information regarding this practice cluster. For many of the assessment Probes, there is not an expectation that a particular model or tool be used. At the diagnostic stage, more information is gathered about your students if you naturally allow students to request tools to use in determining their response and/or in explaining their thinking. An important consideration when using assessment Probes is to combine the use of Probes that expect specific modeling processes or given tools with Probes that expect more varied and open-ended approaches. In this way, you can provide opportunities for students to practice identifying and using helpful tools, and you can learn how their abilities in this area are progressing.

### Assessment Probe Use Related to the Overarching Habits of Mind of Productive Thinkers Practice Cluster

The assessment Probes can support student metacognition by inviting students to identify the extent of their own understanding of a problem and its solution and to examine and make sense of the problem-solving approaches of others. The Probes relate to this overarching cluster of practices both in terms of the content of the Probes and the ways in which they are used in questioning, instruction, and discussion.

### Mathematical Practices Summary

The ideas within the Mathematical Practices must be developed over time and throughout a student's K–12 school experience. "Doing mathematics means generating strategies for solving problems, applying those approaches, seeing if they lead to solutions, and checking to see whether your answers make sense" (Van de Walle, Karp, & Bay-Williams, 2013, p. 13).

## SHARING EXPERIENCES AND PROMOTING PROFESSIONAL COLLABORATION

The engine of improvement, growth, and renewal in a professional learning community is collective inquiry. The people in such a school are relentless in questioning the status quo, seeking new methods, testing those methods, and then reflecting on the results. (DuFour, DuFour, Eaker, & Many, 2006, p. 68)

Using Probes provides an opportunity for collaboration among educators as they examine and discuss student work together:

> The most important aspect of this strategy is that teachers have access to, and then develop for themselves the ability to understand, the content students are struggling with and ways that they, the teachers, can help. Pedagogical content knowledge—that special province of excellent teachers—is absolutely necessary for teachers to maximize their learning as they examine and discuss what students demonstrate they know and do not know. (Loucks-Horsley, Love, Stiles, Mundry, & Hewson, 2003, p. 183)

---

After attending a district-wide workshop on math misconceptions, examining student responses to Probes has become an ongoing part of our bimonthly department meetings. We were intrigued with the student examples shown in the session and were curious about how our own students would respond when given a Probe. Each month, two members of the department, who teach the same course, are responsible for choosing a Probe for the group to analyze. At the first meeting, the pair shares the choice of Probe, giving the rest of us opportunity to do the Probe ourselves and discuss the understandings and possible misunderstandings. We created the following template to guide the discussions.

### Probe: _____

1. What do students need to be able to do and understand in order to answer each item correctly?

2. What does a satisfactory explanation need to include?

3. What misunderstandings are each item likely to target? How might these show up in student explanations?

4. In which courses should we give the Probe?

Before the next meeting, the pair and anyone else who teaches the same course give the Probe to their students. Each of these teachers then chooses four to five examples of student work to bring back to the group: an example with correct reasoning, two to three examples of students with the misunderstandings discussed at the first meeting, and one example of an "unexpected" response. We look at and discuss the student examples and then brainstorm possible instructional ideas, completing the final questions on our template.

5. To what extent were the anticipated misunderstandings a problem in these classes?

6. What additional unexpected misunderstandings were uncovered?

7. What might we do to address these issues?

By providing research sound bites and instructional implications specific to the ideas of the Probe, the Teacher Notes can guide educators through the action research QUEST Cycle, providing a collaborative framework for examining student thinking together and developing plans for improving instruction.

## SUMMARY

An important takeaway about using the Probes is the importance of your role in selecting and scaffolding Probes for use in the classroom. When selecting probes, consider

- how well the content of the Probe aligns to the targeted concepts you want students to learn,
- how well the structure of the Probe lends itself to the mathematical practice you wish students to incorporate, and
- how the Probe will serve as the link between assessment, instruction, and learning.

The first of the considerations, targeting the appropriate math content, was discussed in Chapter 1, where we outlined conceptual and procedural understanding and highlighted where in the Teacher Notes to find information about concepts targeted through a Probe. The second consideration, targeting the ideas within the practices, was the focus of this chapter. The final consideration, providing the link to learning, is a thread that runs throughout the book.

If you are new to using assessment Probes, we suggest that you try a couple of Probes before returning to review the information in this chapter again after you have some firsthand experience. We also encourage you to visit **uncoveringstudentideas.org** to share experiences with others who are using Probes in mathematics and science. We look forward to hearing your ideas.

# Appendix A

## Information on the Standards for Mathematical Practice

> The Standards for Mathematical Practice are not a checklist of teacher to-dos but rather support an environment in which the CCSS for mathematics content standards are enacted and are framed by specific expertise that you can use to help students develop their understanding and application of mathematics. (Zimmermann, Carter, Kanold, & Toncheff, 2012, p. 28)

Formative assessment begins by identifying a learning goal, such as a course expectation from the Common Core State Standards (CCSS). The Common Core State Standards for Mathematics (CCSSM) define what students should understand and be able to do in K–12 mathematics. Since the course expectations in the CCSS define what students should "understand" or "be able to do," it is important for teachers to find out what students know and can do both conceptually or procedurally in relation to the expectation for learning. In addition to these content standards, an important feature of the CCSSM is the Standards for Mathematical Practices. These practices describe a variety of processes, proficiencies, and dispositions that teachers at all grade levels should seek to develop in their students. Since the CCSS do not define the methods and strategies used to determine the readiness and prior knowledge necessary to achieve the standards, the mathematics assessment probes in this book complement CCSS's eight Standards for Mathematical Practices and their link to mathematical content (the preceding information was adapted from Keeley & Rose Tobey, 2011, p. 30).

# STRUCTURING THE MATHEMATICAL PRACTICE STANDARDS

**Figure A.1** The Progression Project's Structure of the Mathematics Standards

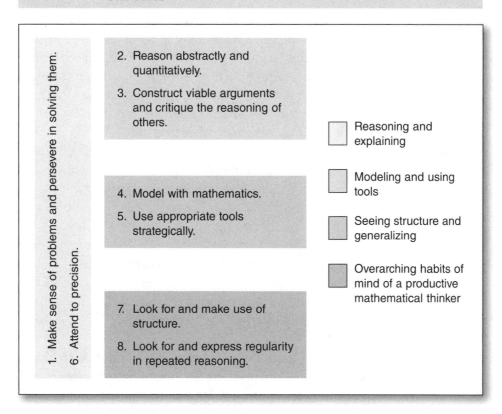

*Source:* McCallum (2011).

The Institute for Mathematics and Education's (IME's) Progression Project is organizing the writing of final versions of the progressions documents for the K–12 Common Core State Standards. The work is being done by members of the original team along with mathematicians and educators not involved in the initial writing of the standards (IME, 2012). The Progression Project created the diagram in Figure A.1 to provide some higher order structure to the practice standards, in the way that the clusters and domains provide higher order structure to the content standards.

The remaining part of this appendix will address each of the Practice Clusters using language from a variety of resources, including the Common Core document and the Common Core Learning Progressions documents. In Chapter 7, we describe how the Probes can be used in relationship to the ideas of each cluster.

## Reasoning and Explaining
## Practice Cluster (Practices 2 and 3)

Each of the Probes includes a selected answer response and an explanation prompt. These explanation prompts are the key to the practices within this cluster.

*Mathematical Practice 2. Reason abstractly and quantitatively.* Students demonstrate proficiency with this practice when they make sense of quantities and relationships while solving tasks. This involves both decontexualizing and contextualizing. When decontextualizing, students need to translate a situation into a numeric or algebraic sentence that models the situation. They represent a wide variety of real-world contexts through the use of real numbers and variables in mathematical expressions, equations, and inequalities. When contextualizing, students need to pull from a task information to determine the mathematics required to solve the problem. For example, after a line is fit through data, students interpret the data by interpreting the slope as a rate of change in the context of the problem.

Students who reason abstractly and quantitatively are able to

- move from context to abstraction and back to context,
- make sense of quantities and their relationships in problem situations,
- use quantitative reasoning that includes creating a coherent representation of the problem at hand,
- consider the units involved,
- attend to the meaning of quantities (not just how to compute with them),
- know and flexibly use different properties of operations and objects, and
- use abstract reasoning when measuring and compare the lengths of objects. (Common Core Standards Writing Team, 2012, 2013a, 2013b, 2013c; Council of Chief State School Officers [CCSSO], 2010)

*Mathematical Practice 3. Construct viable arguments and critique the reasoning of others.* Students demonstrate proficiency with this practice when they accurately use mathematical terms to construct arguments, engage in discussions about problem-solving strategies, examine a variety of problem-solving strategies, and begin to recognize the reasonableness of them, as well as similarities and differences among them. High school students should construct arguments using verbal or written explanations accompanied by expressions, equations, inequalities, models, and graphs, tables, and other data displays, including box plots, dot plots, and histograms. Students should look for examples of correlation being interpreted as cause and sort out why that reasoning is incorrect.

Students who construct viable arguments and critique the reasoning of others are able to

- make conjectures and build a logical progression of statements to explore the truth of their conjectures;
- recognize and use counterexamples;

- justify their conclusions, communicate them to others, and respond to the arguments of others;
- distinguish correct logic or reasoning from that which is flawed and, if there is a flaw in an argument, explain what it is;
- construct arguments using concrete referents such as objects, drawings, diagrams, and actions;
- listen to or read the arguments of others, decide whether they make sense, and ask useful questions to clarify or improve arguments, including, "How did you get that?" "Is that always true?" and "Why does that work?" (CCSSO, 2010; Common Core Standards Writing Team, 2012, 2013a, 2013b, 2013c)

## Seeing Structure and Generalizing Practice Cluster (Practices 7 and 8)

Adolescents make sense of their world by looking for patterns and structure and routines. They learn by integrating new information into cognitive structures they have already developed.

*Mathematical Practice 7. Look for and make use of structure.* Students demonstrate proficiency with this practice when they look for patterns and structures in the number system and other areas of mathematics such as modeling problems involving properties of operations. Students examine patterns in tables and graphs to generate equations and describe relationships. For instance, students recognize proportional relationships that exist in ratio tables, double numbers, graphs, and equations, recognizing the multiplicative properties. Students are expected to see how the structure of an algebraic expression reveals properties of the function it defines. Seeing structure in expressions entails a dynamic view of an algebraic expression, in which potential rearrangements and manipulations are ever present. An important skill for college readiness is the ability to try out possible manipulations mentally without having to carry them out and to see which ones might be fruitful and which are not. In geometry, students compose and decompose two- and three-dimensional figures to solve real-world problems involving area and volume and explore the effects of transformations and describe them in terms of congruence and similarity.

Students who look for and make use of structure are able to

- attend to regularities in numeric table entries and corresponding geometrical regularities in their graphical representations as plotted points;
- see how the structure of an algebraic expression reveals properties of the function it defines;
- develop the practice of writing expressions for functions in ways that reveal the key features of the function;
- measure the attributes of three-dimensional shapes, allowing them to apply area formulas to solve surface area and volume problems; and
- categorize shapes according to properties and characteristics. (CCSSO, 2010; Common Core Standards Writing Team, 2012, 2013a, 2013b, 2013c)

*Mathematical Practice 8. Look for and express regularity in repeated reasoning.* Students demonstrate proficiency with this practice when they look for regularity in problem structures when problem solving, notice if calculations are repeated, look both for general methods and for shortcuts, and use repeated reasoning to understand algorithms and make generalizations about patterns. For example, they make connections between covariance, rates, and representations showing the relationships between quantities. They are expected to move from repeated reasoning with the slope formula to writing equations in various forms for straight lines, rather than memorizing all those forms separately. They use iterative processes to determine more precise rational approximations for irrational numbers. Students justify a statistical hypothesis by simulating the sampling process many times and approximating the chance of a sample proportion.

Students who look for and express regularity in repeated reasoning are able to

- notice if processes are repeated,
- look both for general methods and for shortcuts,
- continually evaluate the reasonableness of their intermediate results, and
- repeat the process of statistical reasoning in a variety of contexts. (CCSSO, 2010; Common Core Standards Writing Team, 2012, 2013a, 2013b, 2013c)

## Modeling and Using Tools
## Practice Cluster (Practices 4 and 5)

Students use different tools (i.e., algebra tiles, graphing calculators, statistical software) in the mathematics classroom. How the tools are used depends on the mathematics topic of focus, and the same tool might be used in a variety of contexts. When given a problem, students need to be able to determine what tool would be appropriate, how the tool could be used in solving the problem, and how to communicate about their process. It is important for students to be able communicate about the modeling process by representing the process using numbers and symbols.

*Mathematical Practice 4. Model with mathematics.* Students demonstrate proficiency with this practice when they model real-life mathematical situations with algebraic equations or inequalities and check to make sure that their equations/inequalities accurately match the problem contexts. For example, students form expressions, equations, or inequalities from real-world contexts and connect symbolic and graphical representations. They explore covariance and represent two or more quantities simultaneously. They use measures of center and variability and data displays (i.e., box plots and histograms) to draw inferences about and make comparisons between data sets. Students use scatterplots to represent data and describe associations between variables. Students need many opportunities to connect and explain the connections between the different representations. They should be able to use all of these representations as appropriate to a problem context.

Students who model with mathematics are able to

- apply what they know to make approximations,
- identify important quantities in a problem situation,
- analyze relationships between quantities, and
- reflect on whether the results make sense. (CCSSO, 2010; Common Core Writing Standards Team, 2012, 2013a, 2013b, 2013c)

*Mathematical Practice 5. Use appropriate tools strategically.* Students demonstrate proficiency with this practice when they access and use tools appropriately. Students consider available tools (including estimation and technology) when solving a mathematical problem and decide when certain tools might be helpful. For example, students might draw pictures, use computer applications or simulations, or write equations to show the relationships between the angles created by a transversal. They may decide to represent figures on the coordinate plane to calculate area. Number lines are used to understand division and to create dot plots, histograms, and box plots to visually compare the center and variability of the data. In addition, students might use physical objects or computer applications to construct nets and calculate the surface area of three-dimensional figures. They make statistical inferences from data collected in sample surveys and in designed experiments, aided by simulation and the technology that affords it.

Students who use appropriate tools strategically are able to

- consider available tools when solving a mathematical problem,
- make sound decisions about when each of these tools might be helpful,
- explain their choice of a particular tool for a given problem, and
- detect possible errors by strategically using estimations. (CCSSO, 2010; Common Core Standards Writing Team, 2012, 2013a, 2013b, 2013c)

## Overarching Habits of Mind of Productive Thinkers Practice Cluster (Practices 1 and 6)

*Productive disposition* refers to the tendency to see sense in mathematics, to perceive it as both useful and worthwhile, to believe that steady effort in learning mathematics pays off, and to see oneself as an effective learner and doer of mathematics. Developing a productive disposition requires frequent opportunities to make sense of mathematics, to recognize the benefits of perseverance, and to experience the rewards of sense making in mathematics. (National Research Council [NRC], 2001, p. 131)

*Mathematical Practice 1. Make sense and persevere in solving problems.* Students demonstrate proficiency with this practice when they make sense of the meaning of the task and find an entry point or a way to start the task. Students solve real-world problems involving ratio, rate, area, and statistics through the application of algebraic and geometric concepts. Students use concrete manipulative, pictorial, and symbolic representations as well as mental mathematics. Students are also expected to persevere while solving tasks; that is, if students reach a point in which they are stuck, they can think about the task in a different way and continue working toward a solution. They may check their thinking by asking themselves, "What is the most efficient way to solve the problem?" "Does this make sense?" and "Can I solve the problem in a different way?" They develop visualization skills connected to their mathematical concepts as they recognize the existence of, and visualize, components of three-dimensional shapes that are not visible from a given viewpoint.

Students who use appropriate tools strategically are able to

- start by explaining to themselves the meaning of a problem and looking for entry points to its solution;
- make conjectures about a solution;
- plan a solution pathway rather than simply jumping into a solution attempt;
- monitor and evaluate their progress and change course if necessary;
- rely on using concrete objects or representations to help conceptualize and solve a problem;
- check their answers to problems using a different method;
- continually ask themselves, "Does this make sense?"; and
- make sense of the problem-solving approaches of others, noticing similarities and differences among approaches. (CCSSO, 2010; Common Core Standards Writing Team, 2012, 2013a, 2013b, 2013c)

*Mathematical Practice 6. Attend to precision.* Students demonstrate proficiency with this practice when they are precise in their communication, calculations, and measurements. Students continue to refine their mathematical communication skills by using clear and precise language in their discussions with others and in their own reasoning. For example, students become more precise when attending to attributes, such as being a special right triangle or a parallelogram. They state precisely the meaning of variables they use when setting up equations, including specifying whether the variable refers to a specific number or to all numbers in some range. During tasks involving number sense, students consider if their answer is reasonable and check their work to ensure the accuracy of solutions. When measuring or using measurement data, students attend to the unit.

Students who attend to precision are able to

- communicate precisely to others;
- use clear definitions in discussion with others and in their own reasoning;
- state the meaning of the symbols they choose, including using the equal sign consistently and appropriately; and
- specify units of measure to clarify the correspondence with quantities in a problem. (CCSSO, 2010; Common Core Standards Writing Team, 2012, 2013a, 2013b, 2013c)

Learn more about how the probes support teachers in assessing ideas related to the mathematical practices in Chapter 7.

# Appendix B

## Developing Assessment Probes

Developing an assessment probe is different from creating appropriate questions for comprehensive diagnostic assessments and summative measures of understanding. The probes in this book were developed using a process similar to that described in *Mathematics Curriculum Topic Study: Bridging the Gap Between Standards and Practice* (Keeley & Rose, 2006; see also Mundry, Keeley, & Rose Tobey, 2012). The process is summarized as follows:

- Use national standards to examine concepts and specific ideas related to a topic. The national standards used to develop the probes for this book are Common Core Standards for Mathematics (CCSSO, 2010). The Common Core Standards for Mathematics (referred to as CCSSM) define what students should understand and be able to do in K–12 mathematics.
- Within a CCSS course expectation, select the specific concepts or ideas you plan to address and identify the relevant research findings. The sources for research findings include the *Research Companion to Principles and Standards for School Mathematics* (National Council of Teachers of Mathematics [NCTM], 2003), *Elementary and Middle School Mathematics: Teaching Developmentally* (Van De Walle, Karp, & Bay-Williams, 2013), articles from NCTM's *Journal for Research in Mathematics Education*, *Second Handbook of Research on Mathematics Teaching and Learning* (Lester, 2007), and additional supplemental articles related to the topic.
- Focus on a concept or a specific idea you plan to address with the probe and identify the related research findings. Keep the targeted concept small enough to assess with a few items as probes are meant to be administered in a short amount of time. Rather than trying to

target as much information about a topic as possible, it is better to be more narrow and focused.

- Choose the type of probe format that lends itself to the situation (see more information on probe format in Chapter 1's "What Is the Structure of a Probe?" beginning on page 13). Develop the stem (the prompt), key (correct response), and distractors (incorrect responses derived from research findings) that match the developmental level of your students.
- Share your assessment probe(s) with colleagues for constructive feedback, pilot with students, and modify as needed.

Feedback on the assessment probes developed for this resource was collected from high school educators across multiple states, and the probes were piloted with students across multiple grade levels in a variety of courses. The feedback and student work were used to revise the probes and to support the development of the accompanying teacher notes.

# Appendix C

## Action Research Reflection Template

### *QUEST Cycle*

### **Q**uestions to Consider About the Key Mathematical Concepts

What is the concept you wish to target? Is the concept at course level or is it a prerequisite?

### **U**ncovering Student Understanding About the Key Concepts

How will you collect information from students (e.g., paper-pencil, interview, student response system)? What form will you use (e.g., one-page Probe, card sort)? Are there adaptations you plan to make? Review the summary of typical student responses.

## Exploring Excerpts From Educational Resources and Related Research

Review the quotes from research about common difficulties related to the Probe. What do you predict to be common understandings and/or misunderstandings for your students?

## Surveying the Prompts and Selected Responses in the Probe

Sort by selected responses and then re-sort by trends in thinking. What common understandings/misunderstandings did the Probe elicit? How do these elicited understandings/misunderstandings compare to those listed in the Teacher Notes?

## Teaching Implications and Considerations

Review the bulleted list and decide how you will take action. What actions did you take? How did you assess the impact of those actions? What are your next steps?

# References

Allen, D. (2007). *Student thinking: Misconceptions in mathematics.* College Station: Texas A&M University. Retrieved from http://www.math.tamu.edu/~snite/MisMath.pdf

Alatorre, S., Cortina, J. L., Sáiz, M., & Méndez, A. (Eds.). (2006). *Proceedings of the Twenty Eighth Annual Meeting of the North American Chapter of the International Group for the Psychology of Mathematics Education* (Vol. 2–23). Mérida, Mexico: Universidad Pedagógica Nacional.

Askew, M., & Wiliam, D. (1995). *Recent research in mathematics education 5–16.* London, UK: HMSO.

Ashlock, R. B. (2006). *Error patterns in computation.* Upper Saddle River, NJ: Pearson.

Black, P., & Harrison, C. (2004). *Science inside the black box: Assessment for learning in the science classroom.* London, UK: NFER/Nelson.

Black, P. Harrison C., Lee, C., Marshall, B., & Wiliam, D. (2004). Working inside the black box: Assessment for learning in the classroom. *Phi Delta Kappan, 86*(1), 8–21.

Bloch, I. (2003). Teaching functions in a graphic milieu: What forms of knowledge enable students to conjecture and prove? *Educational Studies in Mathematics, 52*(1), 3.

Chua, B. L. (2003). *Secondary school students' foundation in mathematics: The case of logarithms.* Singapore: Nanyang Technological University.

Circello, J. E., & Filkins, S. R. (2012). A new perspective on three-dimensional geometry. *Mathematics Teacher, 105*(5), 340–345.

Common Core Standards Writing Team. (2012). *Progressions documents for the common core math standards, draft high school, progression on statistics and probability.* Retrieved from http://ime.math.arizona.edu/progressions/#products

Common Core Standards Writing Team. (2013a). *Progressions documents for the common core math standards, draft high school, progression on algebra.* Retrieved from http://ime.math.arizona.edu/progressions/#products

Common Core Standards Writing Team. (2013b). *Progressions documents for the common core math standards, draft high school, progression on functions.* Retrieved from http://ime.math.arizona.edu/progressions/#products

Common Core Standards Writing Team. (2013c). *Progressions documents for the common core math standards, draft high school, progression on modeling.* Retrieved from http://ime.math.arizona.edu/progressions/#products

Conner, M. E., Rasmussen, C., Zandieh, M., & Smith, M. (2007). *Student understanding of complex numbers.* San Diego State University. Retrieved from http://sigmaa.maa.org/rume/crume2007/papers/conner-rasmussenzandieh-smith.pdf

Council of Chief State School Officers (CCSSO). (2008). *Attributes of effective formative assessment.* Retrieved from http://www.ccsso.org/publications/details.cfm?PublicationID=362

Council of Chief State School Officers (CCSSO). (2010). *Common core state standards.* Retrieved from http://corestandards.org

DeVries, D., & Arnon, I. (2004, July). *Solution—what does it mean? Helping linear algebra students develop the concept while improving research tools.* Paper presented at the 28th Conference of the International Group for the Psychology of Mathematics Education, Bergen, Norway.

Driscoll, M. (1999). *Fostering algebraic thinking: A guide for teachers, Grades 6–10.* Portsmouth, NH: Heinemann.

Driscoll, M., DiMatteo, R. Nikula, J., & Egan, M. (2007). *Fostering geometric thinking: A guide for teachers, Grades 6–10.* Portsmouth, NH: Heinemann.

DuFour, R., DuFour, R, Eaker, R., & Many, T. (2006). *Learning by doing: A handbook for professional learning communities at work.* Bloomington, IN: Solution Tree.

Edwards, M. (2003). Visualizing transformations: matrices, handheld graphing calculators, and computer algebra systems. *Mathematics Teacher, 96*(1), 48.

Elstak, I. (2009). *College students' understanding of rational exponents: A teaching experiment.* Doctoral dissertation, Ohio State University, Columbus.

Garcia, L. (2012). *How to get students talking! Generating math talk that supports math learning.* Retrieved from http://www.mathsolutions.com/documents/How_to_Get_Students_Talking.pdf

Gozde, D., Bas, S., & Erbas, K (2012). *Students' reasoning in quadratic equations with one unknown.* Middle East Technical University. Retrieved form www.cerme7.univ.rzeszow.pl/WG/3/CERME7_WG3_Gozde.pdf

Groth, R. E. (2010). Teachers' construction of learning environments for conditional probability and independence. *International Electronic Journal of Mathematics Education, 5*(1). http://www.iejme.com/012010/d3.pdf

Groth, R. E. (2013). *Teaching mathematics in Grades 6–12: Developing research-based instructional practices.* Thousand Oaks, CA: Sage.

Gür, H. (2009). Trigonometry learning. *New Horizons in Education, 57*(1), 67–80.

Hartweg, K. (2011). Representations and rafts. *Mathematics Teaching in the Middle School, 17*(1), 40–47.

Heritage, M. (2010). *Formative assessment: Making it happen in the classroom.* Thousand Oaks, CA: Corwin.

Institute for Mathematics and Education (IME). (2012). *Progressions documents for the common core math standards.* http://ime.math.arizona.edu/progressions/

Keeley, P. (2012). Misunderstanding misconceptions. *Science Scope, 35*(8), 12–13.

Keeley, P., & Rose Tobey, C. (2011). *Mathematics formative assessment: 75 practical strategies for linking assessment, instruction and learning.* Thousand Oaks, CA: Corwin.

Keeley, P., & Rose, C. (2006). *Mathematics curriculum topic study: Bridging the gap between standards and practice.* Thousand Oaks, CA: Corwin.

Lagasse, A. (2012). *An analysis of differences in approaches to systems of linear equations problems given multiple choice answers.* Durham: University of New Hampshire Scholars' Repository.

Lester, F. K. (Ed.). (2007). *Second handbook of research on mathematics teaching and learning.* Charlotte, NC: Information Age.

Lim Hooi, L., & Wun Thiam, Y. (2012). Assessing algebraic solving ability: A theoretical framework. *International Education Studies, 5*(6), 177–188.

Loucks-Horsley, S., Love, N., Stiles, K., Mundry, S., & Hewson, P. (2003). *Designing professional development for teachers of science and mathematics.* Thousand Oaks, CA: Corwin.

McCallum, B. (2011). *Structuring the mathematical practices.* Retrieved from http:// commoncoretools.me/2011/03/10/structuring-the-mathematical-practices

McTighe, J., & O'Conner, K. (2005). Seven practices for effective learning. *Educational Leadership: Assessment to Promote Learning, 63*(3), 10–17.

Mestre, J. (1989). *Hispanic and Anglo students' misconceptions in mathematics.* East Lansing, MI: National Center for Research on Teacher Learning. (ERIC Document Reproduction Service No. ED313192)

Moore, K. C., LaForest, K., & Kim, H. J. (2012). The unit circle and unit conversions. In S. Brown, S. Larsen, K. Marrongelle, & M. Oehrtman (Eds.), *Proceedings of the Fifteenth Annual Conference on Research in Undergraduate Mathematics Education* (pp. 16–31). Portland, OR: Portland State University. Retrieved from http:// sigmaa.maa.org/rume/crume2012/RUME_Home/Home.html

Moss, C., & Brookhart, S. (2012). *Learning targets: Helping students aim for understanding in today's lesson.* Alexandria, VA: ASCD.

Mundry, S., Keeley, P., & Rose Tobey, C. (2012). *Facilitator's guide to mathematics curriculum topic study.* Thousand Oaks, CA: Corwin.

Muschla, J. A., Muschla, G. R., & Muschla-Berry, E. (2011). *The algebra teacher's guide to reteaching essential concepts and skills: 150 mini-lessons for correcting common mistakes.* San Francisco, CA: Jossey-Bass.

National Council of Teachers of Mathematics. (1999). *Algebraic thinking.* Reston, VA: Author.

National Council of Teachers of Mathematics. (2000). *Principles and standards for school mathematics.* Reston, VA: Author.

National Council of Teachers of Mathematics. (2003). *A research companion to principles and standards for school mathematics.* Reston, VA: Author.

National Research Council (NRC). (2001). *Adding it up: Helping children learn mathematics.* Washington, DC: National Academies Press.

National Research Council (NRC). (2005). *How students learn mathematics in the classroom.* Washington, DC: National Academies Press.

Naylor, S., & Keogh, B. (2000). *Concept cartoons in science education.* Sandbach, UK: Millgate House Education.

Ostler, E. (2013). Exploring logarithms with a ruler. *Mathematics Teacher, 106*(9), 668–673.

Otten, S., Males, L., & Figueras, H. (2008). *Algebra students' simplification of rational expressions.* Michigan State University. Retrieved from https://www.msu .edu/~ottensam/RationalExpression_Simplification.pdf

Pfannkuch, M. (2006). Comparing box plot distributions: A teacher's reasoning. *Statistics Education Research Journal, 5*(2), 27–45.

Poetzel, A., Muskin, J., Munroe, A., & Russell, C. (2012). A journey in visualization. *Mathematics Teacher, 106*(2), 103–107.

Ramirez, A. A. (2009, January 1). *A cognitive approach to solving systems of linear equations.* Ann Arbor, MI: ProQuest LLC.

Resnick, L. (1983). Mathematics and science learning: A new conception. *Science, 220,* 477–478.

Rose Tobey, C., & Fagan, E. (2013). *Uncovering student thinking about mathematics of the common core: Grades K–2: 20 formative assessment probes.* Thousand Oaks, CA: Corwin.

Rose Tobey, C., & Minton, L. (2011). *Uncovering student thinking in mathematics grades K–5: 25 formative assessment probes for the elementary classroom.* Thousand Oaks, CA: Corwin.

Rose, C., & Arline, C. (2009). *Uncovering student thinking in mathematics, Grades 6–12: 30 formative assessment probes for the secondary classroom.* Thousand Oaks, CA: Corwin.

Rose, C., Minton, L., & Arline, C. (2007). *Uncovering student thinking in mathematics: 25 formative assessment probes.* Thousand Oaks, CA: Corwin.

Rubenstein, R. N., & Thompson, D. R. (2001). Learning mathematical symbolism: Challenges and instructional strategies. *Mathematics Teacher, 94*(4), 265.

Satianov, P., Fried, M., & Amit, M. (1999). Broken-line functions with unbroken domains. *Mathematics Teacher, 92*(7), 574–577.

Schwols, A., & Dempsey, K. (2012). *Common core standards for high school mathematics.* Alexandria, VA: ASCD.

Small, M. (2009). *Good questions: Great ways to differentiate mathematics instruction.* New York: Teachers College Press.

Smith, K. B. (1997). Exploration and visualization: Making critical connections about linear systems of equations. *School Science & Mathematics, 97*(1), 749–753.

Stepans, J. I., Schmidt, D. L., Welsh, K. M., Reins, K. J., & Saigo, B. W. (2005). *Teaching for K–12 mathematical understanding using the conceptual change model.* St. Cloud, MN: Saiwood Publications.

Stephens, A. C. (2003). Another look at word problems. *Mathematics Teacher, 96*(1), 63.

Van de Walle, J. A., Karp, K., & Bay-Williams, J. (2013). *Elementary and middle school mathematics Teaching developmentally* (8th ed.). Boston, MA: Pearson.

Van Dyke, F. (2002). *A visual approach to functions.* Emeryville, CA: Key Curriculum Press.

Watson, B., & Konicek, R. (1990). Teaching for conceptual change: Confronting children's experience. *Phi Delta Kappan, 71*(9), 680–684.

Weber, K. (2008). Teaching trigonometric functions: lessons learned from research. *Mathematics Teacher, 102*(2), 144–150.

Wiliam, D. (2011). *Embedded formative assessment.* Bloomington, IN: Solution Tree.

Worrall, L. J., & Quinn, R. J. (2001). Promoting conceptual understanding of matrices. *Mathematics Teacher, 94*(1), 46.

Wylie, E., Gullickson, A. R., Cummings, K. E., Egelson, P. E., Noakes, L. A., Norman, K. M., et al. (2012). *Improving formative assessment practice to empower student learning.* Thousand Oaks, CA: Corwin.

Yetkin, E. (2003). *Student difficulties in learning elementary mathematics.* East Lansing, MI: National Center for Research on Teacher Learning. (ERIC Document Reproduction Service No. ED482727)

Zimmermann, G., Carter, J., Kanold, T., Toncheff, M. (2012). *Common core mathematics in a PLC at work: High school.* Bloomington, IN: Solution Tree Press.

# Index

**230**

# CORWIN

A SAGE Company

The Corwin logo—a raven striding across an open book—represents the union of courage and learning. Corwin is committed to improving education for all learners by publishing books and other professional development resources for those serving the field of PreK–12 education. By providing practical, hands-on materials, Corwin continues to carry out the promise of its motto: **"Helping Educators Do Their Work Better."**